SEAFARING
A CHOSEN PROFESSION

SEAFARING

A CHOSEN PROFESSION

A.F. DICKSON
OBE, RD, FRIN
Extra Master Mariner

JOHN DONALD PUBLISHERS LTD
EDINBURGH

ISBN 0 85976 456 7

A catalogue record for this book is available from
the British Library.

Typeset by WestKey Ltd, Falmouth
Printed and bound in Great Britain by
Cromwell Press, Wiltshire

Preface

The title of this book seems a sensible way of introducing the memories of one who has had a very fortunate and interesting life. I have been extremely lucky. I am slightly dyslexic and I would never have started to write my life story had it not been for my wife's belief that it would be interesting for our children and our grandchildren to have some record of what their father and grandfather had done with his life. Further, I would never have written anything had my daughter-in-law not agreed to translate my dictation into the written word. Never having kept a diary I have had to rely on memory, and I may not have got the various parts in perfect order.

Life has been very kind to me. I had a very happy childhood, and my chosen profession of seafaring suited me very well. I served in destroyers in the Arctic, the Atlantic, the Mediterranean and the Far East and never had a ship sunk under me. After the war I was fortunate to join Shell on the marine side of the business, at a time when my age and qualifications put me in position for interesting jobs and rapid advancement.

By far my greatest good fortune was to marry the most wonderful wife, who had to suffer great difficulty, with husband away and small children to look after. This she did with wonderful efficiency and no complaints at her difficult and often lonely lot.

Our five children, in whom we take great pleasure and pride, have spouses who we love and admire. To complete our happiness we now have ten adorable grandchildren

Kenmore, 1996   A.F.D.

v

Contents

CHAPTER ONE

Early Days

I was born in 1920. I am a Scot, and I suppose in Scottish terms I could be said 'to come of good stock'. My father's antecedents lay with respected and well-known border families—the Pringles, the Cunninghams, the Forrests, as well as the Dicksons. My mother was half Highland and half Lowland; her father came from farming stock in Angus; he was a lawyer and he very unfortunately had a partnership in a law firm in Edinburgh from which his partner embezzled money. My grandfather believed it was his bounden duty to pay back that money and he virtually killed himself trying to pay off the debts resulting from the embezzlement.

My mother's grandfather was a well-known Edinburgh Bailie and there was a jingle that 'Bailie Stott was made to trot off to the Calton jail.' Apparently Bailie Stott was a man of strong views, and he thoroughly disapproved of an annuity tax which the Government had introduced at that time and which he thought was thoroughly unfair because people, particularly people in Scotland, had taken out annuities to see them through their old age, and he felt that that money was virtually sacrosanct. I suppose nowadays it would be unbelievable that anyone would object to any tax on income. However, he did, and he took out an annuity, refused to pay the tax and was sent to the Calton Gaol in Edinburgh.

Apparently this really was his undoing, because all his friends—he was a man who liked good living—sent in huge quantities of both food and drink and the old boy really didn't do himself any good at all, and when he was eventually released from prison didn't survive very long. I have already mentioned that my maternal grandfather suffered financially and my grandmother's family had terrible financial problems also. In addition to the difficulties that befell Bailie Stott the family apparently lost a great deal of money in the failure of the Glasgow Bank. So, taken by and large, I don't think my ancestors, although of very good stock, ever enjoyed wealth to any degree.

I had a very happy childhood in Edinburgh. My mother was left a house by her uncle in a village called Bowriefauld in Angus. It was a very good address—it was called The Hall, Bowriefauld—but it wasn't a spacious house; it was in fact an old co-operative where weavers had lived together in quite small rooms weaving linen. However, it was a very happy place for us and in the early twenties British shipping was very depressed, my father's ship being laid up, and for a while the family lived in the house in Bowriefauld.

We had a pig which rejoiced in the name of Marmaduke, and Marmaduke became a family pet and was a very intelligent animal. It was quite incredible the things that that pig used to get up to. I remember one of the strange things was that it used to pull at my mother's dress until she said, 'Good morning Marmaduke', and then it was quite happy. It was always looking for attention. My father, who was very anxious to try out everything new that was going at that time, bought a motorbike and sidecar. It was a Royal Enfield with a very powerful engine—I think it was 8 horsepower—and he had great difficulty with his bike. He wasn't a very mechanically-minded man and he used to have to try all sorts of tricks to get this motorbike to go. On more than one occasion he had it blocked up on bricks and the pig, Marmaduke, attempting to attract his attention would come along and knock the motorbike off the bricks, much to his disgust.

Looking back on it these must have been very trying and difficult times for my mother and father, because they had two children and my father's income had dried up. They had a certain amount of private money but I don't suppose the interest on the capital could have been very high. However we had, in this Bowriefauld house, a very substantial garden and quite a reasonable greenhouse, so we were able to grow a lot of food and my mother and father were very happy together. My mother was always happy when my father wasn't at sea.

My father, I think, must have had serious worries about his future and the possibility that he wouldn't get another command. I remember a telegram coming to the house intimating that his firm was offering him a ship they had bought—a German ship—called the *Scatwell* which was possibly one of the steamers taken over in reparations from Germany. She was not really a suitable ship for the trade in which the company was engaged—a liner run from Newcastle and Leith to Canada—because she was underpowered for the North Atlantic in the winter. However, my father was only too delighted to get back to sea and he struggled with the *Scatwell* on more than one occasion.

I remember him telling me once that he was on a lee shore with this ship, which seems to have had a pretty limited amount of power—I think her full speed was of the order of 8 knots—and she just would not come out from this lee shore under maximum helm. He said he had only one thing that he could do, which was to turn in towards the shore and swing the ship so fast round to starboard that hopefully she would come out—and she did—but it must have been a very agonising time for my father.

These days in Bowriefauld were very happy. My father's sister in Cults Manse in Fife had six sons and they used to come quite regularly to Bowriefauld, much to my delight. I idolized my elder cousins, and they would take me trout fishing in the little Vinney, a burn just close by. I remember thinking that it was a super little trout stream. I saw it in adult life and I could hardly believe it: it was nothing better than a ditch. My cousins, being much older than me, had the most marvellous motorbikes, and they seemed to me to be absolute heroes.

I believe it had been my mother's idea that my father might be able to find something to do in Angus which would keep him away from the sea, which she hated. But in this she was quite unsuccessful; he loved the sea; he loved the challenge of the North Atlantic; he was a real seaman.

The family moved back to Edinburgh, and my sister and I were both sent to Merchant Company schools. She went to Queen Street, which was called Edinburgh Ladies' College in those days, and I went to Watson's, which was a wonderful school, and I believe I had a very good education of which I didn't take full advantage. The story is told about a lady who, on bringing her young son to Watson's for enrolment, said that she wanted her son to be taken into the class for cabinet ministers. At that time apparently there were a number of Watsonians in the Cabinet; indeed I think that over many years there have nearly always been Watsonians in the Government. The present Secretary of Defence, Malcolm Rifkind, is a Watsonian. In my time at school, however, I am afraid I wasn't really interested in learning. I enjoyed myself and I joined everything in the school. I joined the scouts, I played rugby, not very effectively but very enjoyably, I joined the Officers Training Corps; I was very happy but I was not academically bent and I found the Classics impossible. I studied Latin for seven years and know absolutely no Latin at all now, which is terrible really, because I now realise how important Latin is for those who want to understand the intricacies of complicated grammar. I remember I did rather well at both physics and chemistry because I was interested.

In the late twenties there was another severe depression in British shipping and in the early thirties my father's ship was laid up in the River Tyne. It must have been very hard for my parents in those days, because my father's income dropped off and he managed to stay with the ship, but at a very reduced salary with the ship laid up. There were tiers of ships all lying to buoys, all idle, and in the school holidays during the summer months we all went and lived in the ship. My mother hated it and my sister wasn't very keen, but I loved it. I had a great time. I was able to row the boat ashore for people who came and went, and I used to go up on the bridge and imagine myself at sea in this ship. This was much to my mother's dislike, because she was desperately anxious that I should not follow my father into seagoing.

School fees in those days were nothing like they are now, but they still must have been quite a burden for my parents. Whilst my father didn't really take much interest in what I was doing in the way of education, my mother did, and I think she would really very much have liked me to go to university, but it was pretty obvious that I wasn't going to be able to do that—at least certainly not without a lot of additional expense—and my mother's main intent was to keep me from going to sea.

My father's sister was married to a minister whose charge was the Parish of Cults in Fife. I have already mentioned that they had six sons and a very happy household, and as a boy I was fortunate in spending nearly all my summer holidays there. It was a very happy house and I loved it. My aunt was an incredibly hospitable lady. She seemed to keep open house for all sorts of people. I was always welcome. I didn't realise just how great was the hospitality offered to me when I was a boy, but I do now.

One of my great delights in the summer was to go to harvest fields and chase after rabbits. It is interesting that rabbits can usually run faster than boys, but in the stubble of a harvest field they have a considerable amount of difficulty. It was also a source of income, because, on a really good day I could get perhaps six rabbits from one field, and what I used to do was to thread their legs together, gut them, put them on the cross-bar of my bicycle and cycle four miles to Cupar to the butchers, where, if I was lucky, I could get threepence a pair for these rabbits. This was a great fortune.

I have already said that my academic achievements at school were not of the best, and when I got to the age of 15 my parents had to decide whether it was worth keeping me on at school or whether they ought to try and find something for me to do. As I have said my mother was most anxious that I should not follow my father and go to sea. At that time one of my elder cousins had taken a farm called Tarfachie in Angus and my mother thought that maybe I could become a farmer. My cousin,

Gordon, kindly agreed to take me on as a student. I went to Tarfachie and enjoyed my time there very much. However, I really wasn't cut out to be a farmer. We had the South Esk flowing right past the farm, and at any time on Saturday afternoons I would enjoy fishing in the South Esk or one of the tributary burns, and in the evenings I very much enjoyed shooting rabbits. Once again it was an additional source of income to take these rabbits into Kirriemuir and sell them for what I could get from the butcher because my wage at that time was eight shillings a week—not a lot of money—but I was very well looked after. My cousin Gordon's wife, Betty, was an excellent cook and we lived very well. However, as I have said, I wasn't cut out to be a farmer, and my realisation of this became evident when we were hoeing fields of turnips and I could see the rows stretching, it seemed to me, into eternity. I really didn't feel that that was my thing for the rest of my life. It then happened that my cousin's wife, Betty, was going to produce their first child. She therefore could no longer have somebody in the house, and I had to go.

CHAPTER TWO

The Call of the Sea

I don't know really when I first wanted to go to sea, but I desperately wanted to please my father and I knew that he wanted me to be a sailor and follow in his footsteps. It was therefore agreed that I should, much to my mother's dislike, find myself a seagoing career. I went to Leith Nautical College and did a few months of pre-sea training, and I had an acquaintance in Edinburgh who was a cadet with a Glasgow shipping company. He said they carried a lot of apprentices, so there was quite a happy life on board. The ships were well found and he suggested that I couldn't do better than apply to Patrick Hendersons of Glasgow, which I did.

My first ship, the *Kemmendine*, carried 120 passengers and was on a regular run from Glasgow and Birkenhead to Rangoon. The company, always known as Paddy Hendersons, had six passenger ships and six cargo ships. Cadets always started their career in the passenger ships, and in the later part of their apprenticeship, which in those days was four years they went to the cargo ships. It was a very interesting training and the *Kemmendine* was a happy ship. It was also a very complicated cargo operation. Although the ship carried 120 passengers her real wealth-earning was cargo. The passenger ships loaded on the berth in Queen's Dock, Glasgow, the first tranche of their outward-bound cargo, which consisted of all sorts of things from railway engines to corned beef, and a very considerable amount of whisky and beer. One of the jobs of the apprentices of the ship—cadets as we were called—was to watch the cargo whilst it was being loaded, because the dockers were pretty adept at snaffling a bottle of whisky or any other things that they could get their hands on, and it was quite a job to see what was going on whilst slings of cargo were coming down into the hold and the dockers were stowing the cargo.

The ship was loading cargo in Glasgow and Birkenhead for all her calling ports, which were Gibraltar, Marseilles, Port Said, Suez, Port Sudan, Aden, and sometimes Colombo and Rangoon. Now this was a very complicated operation, because the cargo for all these various ports had to be kept separate, and the separation was made by putting down cargo mats, which were woven palm fronds, and it really was an absolute jigsaw puzzle to load all these various packages of cargo into the hold so that they would all come out in the right order and at the right time. This was a job that was done by very competent stevedores who were used to loading the ships and used to the type of cargo which they normally carried, but the responsibility ultimately lay with the chief officer of the ship. In the *Kemmendine* he was a man called Murdo Ramsay. He was a pretty fierce chap, the scourge of cadets, but he taught me a lot, and I think I got on reasonably well with him. I was anxious to learn and we did a lot of interesting things apart from this dreadful business of watching cargo.

The Captain of the *Kemmendine* was called Plage. He was a square rig master-mariner, and he really didn't believe in the modern sea-going at all. He was a man who still felt that real sailors were people trained in sail, and strangely enough the *Kemmendine* had sails. It seems incredible that a ship like that, carrying passengers out to Rangoon in 1936, should still have sails; but she had, and every time during the voyage these sails were dragged out and set, much to Captain Plage's enjoyment, and then taken down and put away again until the next voyage.

Our second loading port on the outward-bound voyage was Birkenhead on the other side of the Mersey from Liverpool, and that was where the passengers joined the ship.

I remember that during one of my later voyages on the *Kemmendine*, whilst the passengers were coming on board and settling into their cabins a chap wearing a steward's cap went round the passengers, suggesting that there were thieves about, and that it would be a good idea if they gave him any valuables that they might have to ensure their safety. He had a black bag with him into which he put all these valuables, and he said he was going to put them in the ship's safe. Well, he wasn't a steward, and he wasn't going to put them in the ship's safe, and when he had collected a fair number of valuables and quite a lot of money he vanished!

All ships, immediately on arrival in Port Said, were surrounded by bumboat men who came alongside in small boats of all descriptions, their purpose being to sell, preferably to the passengers, if they could, because they had far more money than the ship's company usually had, but they did descend as far as cadets. Cadets didn't have any hard cash. My wage, I remember, for my first year of apprenticeship as a cadet, was £1 a month, which didn't go very far. I nevertheless recollect that you could buy a complete Japanese-made coffee set in Port Said for one shilling and sixpence, so even impecunious people such as I was could do something

7

in the way of getting presents to take home. But that was always done on the homeward-bound voyage and not on the outward bound voyage. On the outward-bound voyage there were other attractions, like Turkish delight and amber cigarette-holders, which we thought were very up-market: these could be purchased by exchanging shirts which our mothers had kindly bought for us!

The trip through the Canal was of interest, obviously, to a first-trip cadet, and it was really a very strange business. The Canal worked throughout the 24 hours, and at night a searchlight was mounted right up on the bows of the ship, its purpose being to illuminate the buoys at the side of the Canal which weren't lit, but which had reflectors, and one of the jobs of the cadets was to work the searchlight. The searchlight which we had on the *Kemmendine* was owned by the company, which was rather unusual. Normally ships hired searchlights from the Canal company but P. Henderson & Co., being a good Scots firm, weren't going to do that, and they supplied their ships with searchlights which worked on an arc principle. The job of the cadet was to adjust the arc, to keep the arc firing in reasonable light, and to adjust the searchlight on the bows of the ship so that it shone accurately down the middle of the Canal and illuminated the buoys on both sides of the waterway.

The common practice was that ships went through the Canal, in those days, in single file, in the order in which they had arrived in Port Said, and ships coming the other way had either to tie up and let you pass, or you had to tie up and let them pass. The *Kemmendine* carried mails and hoisted a Royal Mail flag. One of the advantages of this in the Suez Canal was that she had some degree of preference. Other ships also had preference; for instance, ships carrying dangerous petroleum cargoes—which were, in Suez Canal terms, referred to as 'Benzene' ships—had a right of way over all others because they were regarded as being dangerous.

The trip through the Canal took about 24 hours and very often there was a need to spend some hours anchored in the Bitter Lakes which are roughly half-way along the Canal. There again the ship would be approached by bumboats, but they were mainly selling fruit, and at the right time of year very attractive fruits could be bought—beautiful mangoes—Ismailian mangoes are as good as any in the world. I am a bit of an authority on the subject of mangoes because I love them as a fruit. At other times they had melons or watermelons. All the fruit could be bought in those days very cheaply, and for a few pence you could get a whole basket of mangoes.

Having traversed the Suez Canal we worked cargo in Suez. So as far as the cadets were concerned the whole business of the Canal—Port Said, the Canal itself and Suez—was a very arduous operation, because, as I have said, we had to keep watches on the searchlight all the way through the Canal, and we had to watch cargo at Port Said and Suez. It really was a non-stop business. We were quite glad to get clear of Suez and down into the Red Sea. I have never been a lover of heat, and of course the Red Sea was a dreadful part of the world as far as I was concerned, because it was very hot indeed, and very often you could have a following wind so there was no wind to keep one cool. The way we cooled the cabins in those days was by means of an electric fan which very often didn't work. You also had a wind chute which went through the port hole and stuck out about two feet. Hopefully it brought in some air, but if the ship had a following wind that didn't work at all and it was really very unpleasant.

The next port of call was Port Sudan, which was interesting because the cargo there was worked by 'fuzzy wuzzies' and they really were 'fuzzy wuzzy'. They had hair which stood out about a foot from their heads all the way round, and at the back they had carefully muddied droplets which rattled when they walked. The foremen of the various cargo gangs, of which there was one for each of the holds of the ship, used to choose their men by watching them jump and the chaps who could jump the highest were picked to work the cargo. They were very strong athletic chaps and they could jump a tremendous height from a standing start straight off the deck. The ones who weren't successful just had to retreat, and I imagine that their lot was not a happy one. Another interesting thing about the chaps who worked cargo in Port Sudan was that they were very honest. At the other ports one had to watch the cargo very carefully against the ingenious ways the dockers had of pinching the cargo. They could drop a case of whisky on edge, slacken the box, and remove a bottle. Another trick was to knock a bung out of the barrels of beer we carried, insert a bamboo, and use it as a straw.

The *Kemmendine* had an Indian crew and four European quartermasters. The quartermasters used to wear approximately naval uniform and the Indian crew wore long dungaree-type material shirts, matching trousers with red bands round the midriff, and red caps with a white top. They really looked quite smart when the ship entered harbour. The next port of call after Port Sudan was Aden. It was a brilliant sunny day when we entered Aden and I remember being quite impressed, seeing all these well-dressed Kalassi Indian seamen on the fo'c'sle head of the *Kemmendine* and on the poop, the quartermasters in their smart naval rig, a quartermaster at the wheel, and another quartermaster standing by the various flags. The flags that a ship wore at that time entering harbour were the G flag which meant, 'I require a pilot' and a yellow flag, the Q flag, which indicated a request for *patique*, i.e., a request to enter harbour without any difficulties about the possibility of infection. Aden certainly was not my favourite port, because, as I have said, I don't like the heat, and Aden is a very hot and barren part of the world. However, in those days there was always something to be purchased in any port at which the ship called, and in Aden it was cigarettes. I don't remember the exact value of cigarettes but there was one brand called 'Flag' which was certainly not the best tobacco but had the advantage of being enormously cheap. I think you could get something like 1,000 cigarettes for two shillings.

One of the chief officer's worries in this business of discharging cargo at all the various ports was to ensure that when he arrived in Rangoon, which was the final port of the voyage, he didn't have cargo destined for any of the other intermediate ports. At Aden, which on my first voyage was the last port before Rangoon, there was a great need to search all the holds and make sure that there was no cargo remaining on board that hadn't been discharged as it should have been at any of the intervening ports. Our chief officer, Murdo Ramsay, was very efficient, and he made absolutely sure that everything was in order and that we had no problem.

Arrival at Rangoon meant that all the passengers left the ship and on the evening before arrival at the final destination the passengers were treated to a special dinner. We cadets didn't eat with the passengers but we ate similar food, so we very much looked forward to the final meal where we got rather more luxurious fare than we had on the other days of the voyage.

Whereas we only stayed something like 24 hours in the intervening ports, at Rangoon the ship went alongside a quay, the passengers left, and all of the outward-bound cargo was discharged with the ship lying alongside. It took several days—I don't really remember how many. Then after that, to load the homeward-bound cargo, the ship was taken out to buoys lying in the Irrawaddy River. There the cargo came alongside in barges and the ship worked 24 hours a day. The ship's company were divided into two watches, one from six in the morning to six in the evening, and the other from six in the evening to six in the morning. I always preferred, if I could, to get the night watch, because that was superintended by the second officer who wasn't quite as fierce as the chief officer. Also, we had leave to cook our own meal at twelve midnight, and I developed a taste for cooking which I have had ever since. I used to cook for the second officer and the fourth officer who were the chaps who looked after the working of cargo at night. They discovered that I was quite efficient in the galley, so I was allowed a reasonable amount of time off to do whatever I could with the stores that were allocated to us to make a midnight meal. A disadvantage of the nightwatch was that one had to sleep during the day. In addition to the enormous clatter and noise the day was much much hotter than the night, but it did allow one time to go ashore and do quite a lot of things that could be done in Rangoon. There was a club called the Mayo Marine Club which was a fairly palatial place, supported, I think, to an extent by various charities, where one could enjoy a game of billiards. It was a very pleasant place to have a meal. Then the Seamen's Mission had a place out of Rangoon which could be reached, as far as I remember, by rickshaw where there was a lake and a sailing boat and we very much enjoyed going out there and sailing on the lake.

The homeward-bound cargo was much less interesting. It was bulk cargo, consisting mainly of bran, which was cattlefeed, and teak of all sorts and descriptions—teak planks, railway keys, and also teak logs, which were loaded just as rough logs floated down the Irrawaddy River, brought alongside and hoisted up in slings. They were really enormous and very difficult to stow in a way that filled the ship.

Paddy Henderson's was a very enterprising company and they had all sorts of interests in Burma. They had a company called the Irrawaddy Flotilla Company which ran barges up and down the Irrawaddy and other Burmese rivers. They had interests in the stevedoring companies in Rangoon, and at one time they even had a small airline which carried passengers up to the oilfields at Yenangyaung.

I don't remember exactly how long the stay at Rangoon was, but it must have been a week to ten days. When the ship was finally laden the passengers came on board. We ran to a reasonably exact timing and when the passengers were all on board the homeward-bound voyage began. There weren't nearly as many ports to be visited on the homeward-bound voyage; in fact the only cargo picked up would possibly be fruit in Suez and Port Said. However, the ship usually called at Marseilles on the homeward-bound voyage, so that passengers could avoid the horrors of the Bay of Biscay. Sometimes we also called at Palma in Majorca because the company had an arrangement whereby people could take a voyage out to Palma on an outward-bound ship and a voyage home on a homeward-bound ship and spend however much time they wanted—one or two intervening voyage times—on the Island of Majorca. Quite a popular thing to do in those days. Quite commonly the passenger ships on return to Europe called at continental ports, which might be

11

Amsterdam or Rotterdam, or even occasionally Hamburg, with some part of the homeward-bound cargo.

I made altogether three voyages with the *Kemmendine* and then, as was common, went to one of the cargo ships. The shipping company would like to have employed the cargo ships on a similar trading pattern to the passenger ships. However, at that time there wasn't anything like enough cargo available for them to do that, and a considerable amount of time in the cargo ships was spent carrying bulk cargoes of one kind or another to anywhere in the world—effectively tramping.

The *Arracan* was a very fine old ship and she could, on a good day, do 14 knots, which was quite something for a cargo ship in those days. We got a lot of coal cargoes which were really not very pleasant to carry. They were commonly loaded in South Wales at Barry or Cardiff and it was a pretty horrible business. The coal was brought alongside the ship in railway wagons which were hoisted up on huge loading contrivances, and the whole wagon of coal was then dumped down a chute into the ship's hold. The result of this was that there were swirling clouds of dust everywhere. The whole ship was black; all our clothes were black; everything was covered in coal dust. It was always a pleasure to get the ship out of port and away to sea and get the ship washed down and clean, free once again from this all-pervading coal dust.

But we went to some interesting ports. I remember going to Genoa. Quite often the cargo was not consigned to one receiver with the result that the ship quite commonly had to stay quite a number of days in port discharging small parcels of cargo, and this was true, I remember, of my first voyage to Genoa. We were there for quite a number of days, and we used to enjoy ourselves very much diving off the ship's side into the nice warm harbour waters.

By the time I got to the *Arracan* my remuneration had gone up to £2 a month, so I was comparatively wealthy, to such an extent that it was possible to go to the little restaurants around the harbour and sample the Italian cuisine and the Italian wine. I remember we could purchase at very little cost some wine that we thought was jolly good. On reflection, I think it probably wasn't properly fermented, because it had a considerable tingle about it but it was very palatable and very enjoyable.

About this time the war clouds were beginning to look very ominous over Europe, and my father, who had served in the 1914–18 war in the Royal Naval Reserve in command of a minesweeper, and I, felt that I would like to follow in his footsteps and join the Royal Naval Reserve; I became a probationary midshipman RNR in October 1938. I left the

Arracan to do my first probationary training for midshipman on HMS *Rodney*. I joined the *Rodney* in December 1938.

In those days, the gunnery officers in the Navy regarded themselves as the *corps élite* of the Navy and they used to say that everything led to gunnery and certainly the *Rodney* was very much a gun ship. She had nine sixteen-inch guns in three large turrets on the foredeck. On either side she had three turrets, each with two six-inch guns—her secondary armament. She had four anti-aircraft 4.7s, and four eight-barrelled pom-pom guns. I well remember it being said in those days that aircraft didn't pose any threat, because they would just be shot out of the sky; and of course she could deal with any enemy surface ship which she might encounter. How different it all turned out in real war conditions.

We were given £25 to outfit ourselves to do our probationary training as midshipmen, and we were given a list of required clothing. My mother could see that this wasn't going to work out very well, and instead of going to the recommended naval outfitters she cut some corners, and my best uniform suit, I remember, was bought in Burtons the tailors and my not-so-good one was bought in a shop in Leith which dealt with merchant sailors' clothing. The result was that it was quite obvious that the colour of both my uniform suits wasn't quite right. Looking back on it I think this was very character-forming for me because I had to stand up to a considerable amount of ridicule.

Another problem was that midshipmen in those days wore round jackets, and this wasn't absolutely necessary; but all the other midshipmen had round jackets and I had not. However, I managed to find a round jacket that I could modify in a second-hand shop in Plymouth where I had joined the *Rodney*.

In those days you could buy a considerable number of items from the paymaster's store in the ship, and I could do this against my midshipmen's pay, which was five shillings a day. However, five shillings went quite a long way in those days. You could buy a trenchcoat for twenty-six shillings. I managed, one way or another, to outfit myself, certainly not perfectly, but adequately, to get on with my training. However, I had some strained relations with the Royal Navy midshipmen. There were something like 40 midshipmen altogether in the gun room of *Rodney* and some of these Royal Navy chaps had come straight either from public school or Dartmouth, and they hadn't been around the world as I had been, and I felt myself in some ways to be superior to them. They, on the other hand, felt themselves to be infinitely superior to me. I remember things came to a head. At night, when the ship was in harbour, we used to dine with full regalia, stiff boiled shirts, and our round jackets. *In* *extremis*, I remember one could get round problems of not having a clean shirt by making stiff shirt fronts and cuffs out of menu cards. These had to be held together with a piece of string around the back and over and down each sleeve. It wasn't always easy to keep the whole outfit in place. I remember on one occasion sitting down to dinner in full regalia at a polished table in the gun room of *Rodney*, when I was offered a piece of melba toast by the gun-room steward, which I took, and a midshipman, sitting on the other side of the table, said 'Dickson, if you haven't got any manners when you come here at least you might learn, and it is extremely bad manners to take toast before grace is said', I could feel the back hairs on my neck rising. I was absolutely furious and I said to this chap, 'I don't know where you were brought up, but where I was brought up it was extremely bad manners to contradict or call attention to anybody's shortcomings at table, and I'll accept an apology from you.' This was greeted with hearty laughter all round the table, so I got up from my seat and went and ate my meal at the watchkeeper's table, which had a tablecloth and wasn't subject to any of the formalities attached to the polished table. The following morning I was sent for by the snottie's[*] nurse, the midshipman's guide, philosopher and friend who was a Lieutenant-Commander N, the navigation officer of *Rodney*, and he said, 'Dickson, I imagine that your purpose in joining the Royal Naval Reserve was to find an entry into the Royal Navy, and if you want to join the Navy you will have to behave in a way that is acceptable to your peers.' I replied, 'Sir, I did not have any intention of joining the Royal Navy, and I certainly have no intention now of ever joining the Royal Navy. I will however still be happy to serve in the Royal Naval Reserve during wartime.'

As time wore on I got used to things. I made friends with some of these naval midshipmen, and some of the more difficult ones I got to know in later years, during the war, I found to be perfectly good fellows, but they seemed to me to have been brought up in rather weird surroundings, so that they and I were fish and fowl.

One of the jobs in those days in a battleship which I enjoyed very much was that of midshipman in charge of running a boat. This was a very sensible thing, because it taught one a lot about ship handling. It also taught one a lot about handling men, because one had to look after one's boat crew, and I found that I got on very well with my coxswain and my boat's crew. I think that the Royal Navy had very good man-management training, and a part of that, as far as midshipmen were

---

[*] snottie: naval slang for midshipman

14

concerned, was this business of running boats. I never got into any serious trouble with my running of boats, but I remember that others did, and if you damaged your boat a part of your punishment was that you had to sit by the boat whilst it was being repaired, until it was fit to go back in service. As I say, I never suffered that punishment.

I did suffer quite a severe punishment, however, because one day the ship was doing full-power trials in the Channel and one of the jobs that I had to do was to be midshipman of the watch on the quarter-deck, and in that capacity I was required to run what was called 'the ship's routine'. There was a board which indicated all the things that had to be done, and all that the midshipman had to do. It seemed to me to be a fairly easy duty to tell the marine bugler to make the appropriate call on the ship's loud hailer and call out what the orders were. Steaming up the Channel in a reasonably strong head-wind, I was walking about the quarter-deck with my telescope under my arm, feeling that I was doing a super job, when I noticed that at 4 o'clock I was required to ask the commander's permission to call 'evening quarters,' which meant that all the marines and sailors had to turn up on deck in their various divisions and be inspected. So I went down to the commander's cabin. The commander was having an afternoon caulk, (nap), so I woke him and said, 'Sir, do you wish me to sound off 'evening quarters'?' He replied, 'What's the weather like?' and I said, 'It's fine.' So he announced, 'Right, sound off evening quarters'. Now that was a very bad mistake, because, although the weather was fine on the quarter-deck, it wasn't fine on the forepart of the ship, where there was a considerable amount of spray coming over, and when the commander came up to conduct his evening quarters the first thing that happened when he went round the side of the screen at the afterpart of the ship was that one of the sailor's caps came rolling along at his feet, and the sailors were in complete disorder; they'd doubled up through the hatches into this spray and wind on the forepart of the ship. The commander was not best pleased, and he said, 'Dickson, you think it was a good day do you?' and I was stupid enough to respond, 'Well, I had thought so sir'. He said, 'Right, get up on the top of B turret' (which was a superimposed turret, the highest gun turret on the forepart of the ship) 'and stay there until I tell you to come down.' I was dressed only in a round jacket—a most unsuitable garb for standing on the top of a gun turret in a ship coming up-channel at full speed in a nasty half-gale of wind. I was left there until I was absolutely frozen stiff, soaked to the skin. However I suppose it did teach me some sort of a lesson!

The *Rodney* went down to Gibraltar to join in combined fleet manoeuvres with the Mediterranean fleet, and what a sight Gibraltar was in those days. There were squadrons of battleships; many squadrons of cruisers were lying in the bay outside Gibraltar harbour, and the harbour itself was absolutely full of flotilla after flotilla of destroyers. What a stirring occasion it was to see all these magnificent ships leaving harbour and forming up to conduct these enormous manoeuvres. And what a dreadful headache it was for midshipmen when the ships were in harbour, because many of the senior officers' wives had come down to Gibraltar and, particularly on Sunday mornings, they would come off to join their husbands. As I've said, one of the jobs of midshipmen was to run boats. Whereas the senior naval officers were very difficult, their wives were even more difficult and were also very conscious of their seniority. Mere midshipmen were easy targets for their annoyance when things didn't go quite as they felt they should.

After the combined fleet manoeuvres *Rodney* went down to Madeira, showing the flag, and a party was arranged for all the Portuguese dignitaries. There was to be a Royal Marine band and dancing on the quarter-deck, which was an appalling thought as far as I was concerned. I therefore managed to get myself appointed as midshipman of the watch when the guests were arriving, which I felt would keep me in a position of reasonable safety from the festivities. However I couldn't have been more wrong, because the last people to arrive were the Portuguese Captain of the Port and his wife, and two rather plump daughters; I was instructed to take them down to the captain's cabin. The captain was a man called Syfret who later became a very distinguished Admiral in the Royal Navy. To my horror he asked me to remain in his cabin and have a glass of sherry with the young ladies, the daughters of the Captain of the Port. After we had had our glass of sherry he said, 'Midshipman, will you please instruct the marine bandmaster to commence playing, and will you take the elder daughter and lead off the dance?' I can remember yet my absolute horror at having to obey this direct order, and I had to stumble around on the quarter-deck. Fortunately a number of the officers saw my distress, and they got partners and joined in the dancing, so that I was able to more or less hide myself.

Notwithstanding all my difficulties, my rank as a midshipman in the Royal Naval Reserve was confirmed as a result of my training in *Rodney*, and I went back to the merchant service, back to Paddy Henderson's, and joined a ship called the *Henzada*. She had been built by the company in the time of fairly severe recession (or 'depression', as it was called in those days) and she was not of the same quality as the old *Arracan*. She could only do eight knots, and she burned eight tons of coal a day; she could carry 8,000 tons of cargo, so she was an eight, eight and eight ship.

The fact that the *Henzada* could only do eight knots had an advantage as far as I was concerned, because eight knots was a speed at which you could fish from the ship, and catch tuna, fish dolphin, and other fast-swimming fish. It was really quite an easy thing to do, and we cadets used to arrange a rather complicated set of ropes. The first thing we did was to have a length of sounding wire, which was fairly fine wire with a huge hook on it, baited simply with various colours of cloth. That was attached to a log line which was rove through a block at the end of a boom at the after-end of the ship and brought inboard. It was an upright with a small ship's fender on it attached with a trigger of sail twine to the log line trailing over the ship's stern. If a fish took the bait the fender fell down, and that could be seen from the bridge. The captain was fairly accommodating to us in our endeavours to catch fish, and if the fender fell the officer of the watch was instructed to stop the ship and we were called to pull in the fish; it was very nice to have fresh fish to eat.

Time in the *Henzada* was not to be very lengthy. War broke out in September and I was immediately called up. My first appointment was to go to Kirkwall.

17

CHAPTER THREE

In Time of War

Reporting to Kirkwall to the senior naval officer, another Royal Naval Reserve midshipman and I were instructed to take ourselves off to the Queens Hotel in the town, where we were allocated a bedroom. I remember that the chambermaid said to us, 'Would you gentlemen like your breakfast in bed?' I remember he and I being woken up at about eight o'clock in the morning and this charming chambermaid bringing in our breakfast on two trays and I remember thinking, 'Well, if this is war, it's all right.'

We weren't there very long because, on 16 September we were both sent to join a cruiser, HMS *Delhi*—a beautiful old ship. She was engaged in the Northern Patrol, and our *raison d'être* in the ship was to act as boarding officers. Boarding really was quite a terrifying operation. The whole squadron of cruisers took up station within horizon-sighting distance apart, so that, spread out south of Iceland they provided a screen more or less across the trade routes of the Northern Atlantic. If a neutral merchant ship was sighted she was instructed to stop. A boat was lowered from the cruiser, and a party was dispatched to the ship. If it was thought that there was any doubt about the final destination of the cargo the ship would be sent in for contraband control, as it was called, in Kirkwall.

This was, of course, in winter, and boarding ships in the middle of the Atlantic in winter is not really a thing to be recommended, particularly at night. It involved dropping a cutter from the cruiser's davits, rowing over to the merchant ship, boarding the merchant ship by pilot ladder, and deciding then whether the ship had to be taken into Kirkwall or not. In fact, virtually all neutral ships had to be taken into Kirkwall, and a midshipman, together with a petty officer and six seamen, formed the boarding party, to ensure that the ship complied with their instructions.

The commander of the *Delhi* was a very pusser (punctillious) naval officer, and he instructed me that the proper rig for boarding officers in wartime was naval gaiters, boots, a cutlass, a revolver, 36 rounds of ammunition, and suitable charts. So on my first occasion, dressed in all this stuff, with the added burden of a naval greatcoat because it was pretty cold, off I went in the cutter to board my first ship. The weather was pretty terrible, pitch dark, snowing, wind force 7, and the ship that I had to board was rolling very heavily and the pilot ladder was not as pilot ladders are today, but such that the steps could all go flat against the ship's side; when I was half-way up, complete with boots, cutlass, and all the rest of it, this is exactly what happened. I was left clinging on to the ship's side with virtually nothing to hang on to, and at the next roll of the ship I fell off the ladder. Fortunately one of the chaps in the cutter caught hold of me, although I was well down into the Atlantic by the time he managed to grab me and save my life. I did eventually manage to board the ship, soaking wet, and I did take her into Kirkwall. That wasn't always an easy task, but I found what I thought was a sensible way of dealing with the problem. What I did was to draw on the chart of the merchant ship imaginary minefields, leaving him a gap which he could sail through, which took me very close to Noop Head, the Northern Light in the Orkney Isles. From there I reckoned I could get to Kirkwall without too much bother. This worked like a treat. I remember one other midshipman less fortunate than myself, running his ship ashore on the Orkney Islands and sending a signal to the Senior Naval officer, Kirkwall, saying, 'I am ashore, position unknown, please send assistance?', which obviously didn't get him any good marks.

Looking back, it's quite extraordinary that midshipmen, such as I, who had virtually no experience whatsoever, were entrusted with these duties. It does seem very odd. I think I was very fortunate in that there was a Lieutenant, RNR, in *Delhi* who had been Chief Officer of the *Discovery*. He was a very fine seaman, and he rigged up a short mast about six feet, and a little triangle of sail, which greatly helped the cutter in very severe weather to lie to the wind. If the merchant ship was kind enough to give us a lea, which they didn't always do, then it was much easier to get alongside them and board with this rig that the RNR lieutenant had fixed up in the cutter. I think my second ship was a Norwegian tanker laden with a full cargo of motor gasoline, and she was a fine new ship. By that time I had discarded the boots, the gaiters, and cutlass, and all that stuff, and I simply boarded the ship in trousers, roll top sweater, with a revolver in the waistband of my trousers, and gym shoes. It was much easier to get up ladders with that sort of rig, and I could get the rest of my stuff aboard the ship with a bag.

I remember I was up on the bridge with the captain, and we were watching another Scandinavian ship quite a long way ahead of us with all her lights on. All of a sudden up she went. The Captain said, 'What do you think we should do?' I was really in no position to advise him. I suggested he might put the lights out and turn 90 degrees to port, which is what he did. We had no further trouble. The following morning we resumed course for Noop Head. I had to adjust my minefields a little, bit but that didn't seem to give too much trouble.

Delhi was a very happy ship, as far as I was concerned. She had no gun room, so we midshipmen—there were two RNR midshipmen and the Captain's secretary was an RN midshipman paymaster—lived in the ward room. It was very interesting, because quite a number of the senior officers in the ship had been axed or had left the Navy for one reason or another. They had been in all sorts of employment and were very interesting people to talk to; we had a bridge four and there was quite a lot of chess played. I enjoyed it very much.

It was interesting that the Navy at that time hadn't really got used to wartime. They still used to have dinners with mess kit and I remember on one occasion the Captain, L.H.K. Hamilton, was invited to dine in the mess in the ward room with the Royal Marine Band playing outside. It was all very splendid. Captain Hamilton was a very fine naval officer; he eventually became an Admiral, and I ran across him later when he was in command of the covering force for a Russian Convoy (PQ17) of which I will write about in detail in a later chapter.

During my time in the *Delhi* I did not see any enemy action. I do, however, remember that there was a report of a heavy German ship breaking out into the Atlantic to raid the North Atlantic convoys. I recall Captain Hamilton coming up to the bridge on receipt of a signal from the Admiralty and saying quite quietly 'full speed ahead, both engines.' The ship was closed up at action stations all night. *Delhi* had six torpedoes on each side, and the Captain made clear his intent to attack with torpedoes if we sighted the enemy. This was very exciting for me, because my action station was the starboard torpedo tubes. However, perhaps fortunately, we did not sight the German ship.

The practice for boarding officers was that having taken a ship into Kirkwall they joined a guard ship which in due course sailed up to Sullom Voe which was the base for the cruisers. My first trip up to Sullom Voe was in a converted Isle of Man packet called HMS *Manx Maid*. The ship entered Sullom Voe just at lunchtime when the first air raid on the British Isles took place. The first thing we knew about it was when the *Manx Maid's* three-inch gun went into action. Mounted on a sponson (a steel tube going down one or more decks) which went through the ward-room table, it had sufficient recoil to crack the table!

The raid did no damage but a rabbit was killed and it, or perhaps another just like it, was produced in the Windmill Theatre in London.

About the turn of the year the Admiralty, in their wisdom, decided that the *Delhi* should be converted to an anti-aircraft cruiser, so the ship was paid off and I left her in January 1940.

CHAPTER FOUR

Destroyers

My next appointment after leaving the *Delhi* was to join the Destroyer *Keppel*, my favourite ship. She was at that time in Malta, being repaired after a collision with a French destroyer in the Bay of Biscay. I took passage out to Malta to join the ship in a B1 Ship called the *Modassa*. *Keppel* was a fine old ship. She was laid down in 1919 but not completed until 1925. She was a flotilla leader with five 4.7 guns, six torpedoes and a 3-inch anti-aircraft gun. During my time in Malta, whilst the ship was still in dry dock, I was sent to the navigation school in the dockyard, which was very useful to me in later life as I learned quite a lot of navigation at that time. Malta was generally a very happy time for me. The sub-lieutenant and I managed, between us, to hire a car on a number of occasions, and went all round the Island—a very interesting island, indeed.

The *Keppel* was in fact at that time based in Gibraltar. Captain D. Thirteen, the Captain in charge of the thirteenth flotilla, had decided that he could serve his flotilla best by being stationed ashore in Gibraltar, and so in the main *Keppel* operated as a private ship, i.e., a ship not carrying anyone in charge of the flotilla, under the command of Lieutenant-Commander Heywood Lonsdale. We left Malta after completion of the repairs, and on the way back to Gibraltar there were other ships of the flotilla with us. It was then that I had my first taste of manoeuvring a destroyer in close order, which is a very exciting and interesting exercise for a young man. Destroyers are very fast and fine ships to handle and they manoeuvre very precisely in close order; it's a great thing for a young chap to be a watch keeper in a destroyer.

When we arrived in Gibraltar our normal business was to patrol the Straits because the Admiralty were anxious to prevent German U-boats operating in the Atlantic from entering the Mediterranean. There were a number of patrol areas manned by the various destroyers in the flotilla. Normally we spent about a week or ten days on patrol, returning to Gibraltar to bunker and restore the ship.

The war, of course, at this time was not going well in North Europe, and eventually France collapsed under the German invasion. The

Admiralty then decided that they would have to take some action to prevent the French fleet, largely in Oran, from falling into the hands of the Germans, because Algiers seemed to be rather Vichy orientated. A fleet, under the command of Admiral Bruce Fraser, was therefore sent to Oran under Admiralty instructions to negotiate with the French Command in order to persuade the French fleet to surrender and come over to our side, or at the very worst to remain neutral and give undertakings to that effect. Should the French not agree Fraser was to engage the French ships. The thirteenth destroyer flotilla, with *Keppel* as leader, were responsible for screening the British fleet against U-boat attack, which meant that Captain D. and his staff were all embarked on the ship. Bad news for me—because, as the most junior officer on the ship I immediately lost my cabin and I had to sling a hammock which I hadn't done for quite a long time.

Of course, the ship was buzzing with specialist officers who were the staff officers of Captain D., a flag lieutenant, a gunnery officer, a torpedo officer, a navigating officer, and so on. *Keppel* carried a captain, Captain Plaidell Bouvrais, who had a very competent command of the French language and he was entrusted with the task of negotiating with the Admiral in charge of the French fleet to investigate the best method of implementing the Admiralty's intent to ensure that the French ships didn't come under German control.

Keppel went close into the entrance to the harbour of Oran, and Captain Plaidell Bouvrais went in the ship's launch into the harbour to carry out his negotiations with the French admiral. I remember this being about the middle of the day, and I think the deadline for the French was fairly early in the afternoon. Captain Plaidell Bouvrais in due course returned to the ship, saying that his negotiations with the French had been unsuccessful; after the expiry of the deadline, the time of which I certainly don't remember, we opened fire. The battleships far offshore opened fire on the French fleet. *Keppel's* guns were well out of range. The French replied, and it was my first experience of enemy shellfire. The shellfire, of course, was not directed against the destroyers, but rather against the heavy ships of the fleet and it was not very successful. I don't think any hits at all were made on British ships. One quite striking thing was that the French shells produced various colours of splashes in the water, bright green and bright red, this being so that the various gunners in the French ships could see their own shells and identify them, as opposed to those from other ships. In the event, the French ships being in harbour and seriously hampered, their gunnery was not really up to much, and they sustained very serious damage. The action, as far as the British were concerned, was a success, in that the French ships were irreparably damaged and certainly would be of no use to the Germans.

Our next task was to go to the two French ports in Southern France, Cette and Port Vendres, to evacuate Polish and Czech troops from these two ports. To effect the evacuation British merchant ships in the Mediterranean were diverted into the ports, the idea being that the Czech and Polish troops, together with their equipment, would be loaded onto these ships, and the ships would then set sail for Gibraltar. This experience taught me a very great deal about what happens when law and order collapses. The situation in France at that time was that nobody really quite knew what was happening. The government of France had collapsed, they had capitulated and signed a peace treaty with Nazi Germany, but nobody knew what the effect of that would be in the South of France. It was assumed that German troops would arrive at any time. There was much tension and concern, and I came to realise that once civil authority collapses, as it had in that part of France, the rule of the gun is what prevails: the Polish and Czech troops that we were sent to evacuate were taking what they wanted from the French civil population and the situation really was quite chaotic. I remember that when we were lying alongside, in the harbour at Port Vendres, a large number of refugees from various parts of Southern France had gathered there, in the hope of evacuation: many were virtually starving, and the sailors in *Keppel*, seeing what was happening, reacted in the way that British sailors always would, and tried to do something to help the people that were in trouble. I remember seeing the sailors at their dinner-time taking their mess trays ashore and letting the people help themselves to *their* dinners. It was quite astonishing to see elegant persons, ladies with beautifully manicured nails and expensive rings on their fingers, scrabbling about in the sailors' mess-tins, trying to get something to eat.

Of course *Keppel* had some difficulties in obtaining our provisions, and I remember being dispatched with a party of blue jackets and a large quantity of French money. I can't remember the amount, but it seemed to me to be very considerable. My instructions were to go and get some meat. The shops in the little town were all shut and the people were obviously not prepared to deal in normal trading conditions. However, I just went to the butcher's shop, and we hammered on the door with rifle butts. Eventually, the butcher came and we told him that we were going to buy his meat and he didn't really have any option in the matter. We put this large quantity of French money on the counter and helped ourselves and took the meat back to the ship. Of course I think that news of the action on the other side of the Mediterranean had got to France and there was a certain amount of hostility, which is quite understandable, and I remember on one occasion the French local authorities posted a machine-gun picket on the ship's gangway, and said that they weren't going to allow anything that they didn't like to go on. Lieutenant-Commander Heywood Lonsdale's response to this was to train the ship's 4.7's on the *Guildhall* and make it known that if there were any shots to be fired then the *Guildhall* wouldn't come out too well.

Another of the extraordinary duties that I remember befell me was that I was told to go and assume some duties as British Consul in the Consulate. I think that was in Cette. I had no idea of what that amounted to but I found the Consulate and did virtually nothing other than to sit in an office and pretend to be capable of dealing with anything that might come along. On the whole the operation was really quite successful. We got a large number of troops and a very considerable amount of equipment loaded onto various merchant ships and there was an Egyptian flag passenger ship lying off. I think her name was the *Kedive Ismael*, and she was too large to enter the harbour. She did, however, provide obviously good accommodation for the troops, and *Keppel* was used as a tender, taking troops off to this passenger ship. In due time the whole armada sailed back to Gibraltar.

Another interesting thing as far as I was concerned was that information arrived in Gibraltar to the effect that a Danish salvage tug stationed in Lisbon was prepared to be taken prize by the British Navy. The contacts with the Danish salvage tug indicated that some of the crew weren't entirely happy with this arrangement. However, the Captain was very keen indeed that his ship should come over to the allied side in the war, Denmark at that time having been occupied by Nazi troops. Our rendezvous position was arranged, *Keppel* in due time making the rendezvous, while I was instructed to take the ship as a prize of war into Gibraltar. Remembering my lessons of the northern patrol and the weather being fine, I was able to board the ship in full boarding kit—gaiters, cutlass, revolver, and all the rest of it—with a party of six blue-jackets. One of the instructions in the Admiralty procedures for taking a prize of war was that all valuables were to be agreed and put in charge of the officer of the prize crew; particular mention was made of gold. It was rather amusing that on boarding this ship the Captain received us in his cabin, smiled, and revealed a complete set of gold teeth. The First-Lieutenant of the *Keppel* had come with me to go through the formalities of taking the ship as a prize. He was a very serious-minded chap and he insisted that in the affidavit of valuables which had to be completed when the ship was taken as a prize should include the Captain's teeth. After the completion of all the various formalities the ship's boat with the First-Lieutenant left, and off I went with my prize. I can remember standing on the bridge in the bright sunshine feeling very proud of myself; I was nineteen years old and this was my first command. Although I was very conscious of the fact that we had information that some members of the ship's crew were not entirely happy about being taken prize it didn't seem to me that we had too much to worry about, because I had six strapping sailors with me, all armed, and I couldn't really see much of a problem.

So I was walking up and down on the bridge of my prize thinking that life was pretty good, when I became conscious of the fact that the weather was worsening all the time from the north-west, and by nightfall we were in half a gale of wind and weather deteriorating: it really looked quite nasty. I can remember beginning to be a bit concerned about the safety of the ship on her heading with a heavy following sea developing and to my horror I realised that the whole of the after-deck of this ship was practically taken up with hatches to the engine room, and these hatches were all open. I said to the Captain, 'I don't know how you run these ships in heavy weather, but the weather's getting worse all the time and she's taking a lot of water over the after-deck. It seems to me that a great deal of it is going straight down into the engine room. How do you feel about this?' The Captain said, 'Well, that's perfectly normal.' However I wasn't entirely happy and I thought I would go down to the engine room where I learned that the fellows keeping watch there were quite happy about everything! They were dressed like seamen, wearing oilskins, and the water was sloshing about all over the place. But they, of course, had an enormous amount of pumping capacity from the ship's salvage operations, and they didn't seem to be bothered so I imagined that it would be all right. So back I went to the bridge, intending simply to ensure that the ship stayed on her course, and that nothing untoward came about. We were making quite a reasonable speed in the direction of the Straits of Gibraltar and all I really had to do was to have a seaman keep watch. We set watches and the seaman on watch had to ensure that the ship maintained her course. In due time I was in the happy position of sailing the ship into Gibraltar harbour with the white Ensign flying above the Danish Ensign. I got alongside the jetty in Gibraltar and went to deliver the vessel to the naval authorities. I remember saying to the Lieutenant-Commander in charge of the appropriate authority in Gibraltar, 'I think I should have a receipt for this tug', and he solemnly wrote out a receipt: 'Received from Midshipman A.F. Dickson, one tug'.

I kept that piece of paper for quite a long time and then I lost it. I was looking for it but I can't find it.

Strangely enough, I became friendly with a Danish chap later on in my Shell life. We became not only business friends but social friends, and one of his chums in Denmark was a director of this salvage company that had in fact owned the *Valkyrie* when he was a young chap, and he was very interested to know that I was the one who had taken his ship prize during the early part of the war.

About the middle of 1940 the thirteenth destroyer flotilla was ordered back to the United Kingdom, and I remember we came into Portsmouth where the ship was visited by King George VI. Many of the *Keppel's* crew were postmen; they were sailors who had served their full 12 years in the navy, but had stayed on the retired list and were called up and called back to the colours on the outbreak of war. I remember the King was very interested in the fact that a number of the sailors in the ship were wearing postmen's trousers, because these chaps had got jobs as postmen when they left the navy. The King had arrived so suddenly alongside the ship that the First-Lieutenant didn't have time to get his crew all smartened up. The King then remarked on the fact that it was unusual to see sailors with a red stripe down the side of their trousers.

Keppel then went up to Greenock and Lieutenant-Commander Heywood Lonsdale was relieved by a four-stripe Captain, Captain Donald K. Bain, who was a typical destroyer officer of the old school. He was an extreme disciplinarian, a bit of a martinet, and a very tough chap to serve. He very soon came to the same conclusion as Captain De Winton had in Gibraltar that he could run his operations better from the shore than he could from staying in the ship, and he took his staff ashore at Greenock. *Keppel* was then operating from Greenock on North Atlantic convoy duty.

So once again *Keppel* became a private ship under the command of the First-Lieutenant, Lieutenant Hanson. We operated out of Greenock for a number of months, but the Admiralty were at this time conscious of the fact that the convoy problems—the problems of getting merchant ships safely across the Atlantic—were becoming fairly acute, and that the problem of escorting these convoys would have to be given much more attention than hitherto. It was decided that the convoy escort base should be shifted from Greenock and Liverpool to Londonderry. Escort groups were formed in Londonderry and *Keppel* became the leader of the first escort group, while Commander A.M. Sheffield was appointed as Commander of the first escort group, and captained *Keppel*. Shorty Sheffield, as he was always known in the Navy, was another fierce destroyer officer, a strict disciplinarian and a bit of a martinet. I liked him, and I think I got on reasonably well with him. By this time I was a Sub-Lieutenant in charge of one of the watches on the ship, and I began to regard myself as a fairly experienced destroyer officer.

Keppel and ships of her type had been built from experience of the 1914–18 war and they were really designed for operations in the North Sea. Of course our convoy duties were largely, in fact almost exclusively, in the North Atlantic, which is a very different proposition indeed, and whilst I suppose the ships were safe enough they certainly were extremely uncomfortable in the North Atlantic in winter time. I remember there was a considerable push at that time that the Navy should liaise closely with the coastal command, and we were operating with aircraft from Limavady in Northern Ireland which is quite close to Londonderry. Some RAF officers were set to go out with this typical convoy and I remember on one bright moonlit night when the weather was quite quiet and peaceful these RAF officers were on the bridge of the ship. It must have been, I suppose, first watch at night, somewhere between eight and midnight, and there were a lot of fish noises on the asdic—high-pitched screaming that got louder and louder and louder and then sort of died away again. These RAF chaps, obviously a bit nervous about the whole thing, said, 'What the hell is that?' and we said, 'Oh dearie me that's torpedo noise', and they were not amused at all; we took great pleasure in watching their discomfort. Eventually, of course, we told them that what we had been telling them were torpedoes were in fact dolphins, and they took it all in very good part—or at least we thought they did. In due time the wardroom of *Keppel* were invited to go to Limavady to fly with these chaps, who were then operating twin-engine aircraft called Hudsons which were converted American passenger planes. That wasn't my first flight with the RAF, but I think it was my second of the war, and I didn't like flying very much. Certainly these Hudsons weren't really very comfortable except for those who had properly accommodated seats and proper flying gear. This other naval man and I were simply there in naval uniform, standing in the centre of the aircraft with nothing to do except either sit on the body of the plane with no seat, or stand up feeling uncomfortable and very cold. We didn't enjoy it too much, and when we got out to about the limit of the patrol that this aircraft was on it was quite obvious that things weren't as they should be. One of the engines, I think the starboard one, was 'feathered', and one of the RAF men came and said, 'Look, we're terribly sorry about this, but we've lost the starboard engine.' Well, we knew that there had been something wrong and we said, 'Well, that's OK; presumably we can fly on one.' They replied 'Well, yes we can for quite a long time, but there is no way we can get back to base on one engine.' That wasn't very good news, and at that time, it seems incredible now, but at that time the aircraft in the RAF carried two pigeons which they could use to send messages *in extremis* and these pigeons, I can see them yet, were in wire-netting cages in the aircraft, and the fellows said, 'Well, look you chaps, we are all going to write messages to our mothers and perhaps you would like to write messages to your mothers.' The special paper for this was rather like cigarette paper that could be folded and put into a little silver capsule on the pigeon's foot. So this other chap and I sat solemnly and rather dolefully composing messages to our mothers saying that things weren't so good but we loved them dearly and when all this routine was completed they switched on the starboard engine again. By that time the aircraft was down about 100 feet above the sea and we really weren't feeling good at all. The RAF chaps said 'Well that will teach you to have us on with all that torpedo business,' which I suppose was 'fair-do', and of course in due time we arrived back perfectly safely at the RAF station in Limavady.

The only other thing I remember about Commander Sheffield's command of the ship was that we had on one occasion to go down the east coast of England; I think we were going to refit somewhere on the Thames. The east coast, of course, was subject to a lot of enemy air activity, and one afternoon when I was on watch an aircraft came out of the sun, and without too much clue of what it might be I opened fire. There is nothing that brings the captain of a destroyer to the bridge more quickly than a 4.7 going off at high angle just outside his sea cabin, and Shorty Sheffield arrived on the bridge of *Keppel* just in time to see a plane with the RAF roundels on the wings pass over the bridge, having been fired on. He was very cross and ordered me off the bridge, saying I was a disgrace to the service and would be relieved of my watch-keeping duties until further notice. I was not best pleased, since I thought that the aircraft had made no recognition signals, had come out of the sun, and I really didn't have too much of an option. I must say I give full marks to Commander Sheffield, because, when the ship eventually arrived down on the Thames, I think we then de-ammunitioned ready for a fairly major overhaul. Before leaving the ship and giving leave he was doing what many destroyer captains did in those days—wishing the crew a good leave. He cleared lower deck to do this, and he was kind enough to say that he had been wrong in relieving me of my duties as Officer Watch, and he had acted quite understandably on his arrival on the bridge, seeing that we had opened fire on a British aircraft; but he did say that, as Officer Watch I really didn't have any option, with the aircraft coming out of the sun as it had, with no rendition signal. I really had no option but to open fire.

Ships at this time of the war were refitted with maximum dispatch, and in no time flat we were back in Londonderry—back on the North Atlantic convoy duties. Being the escort group with the largest number of destroyers in the group we did a lot of fast escort duty, i.e., the fast troop ships going across the Atlantic, the *Queen Elizabeth* and the *Queen Mary*. They were very difficult ships to escort because they went at high speed and that was their best defence against U-boat attack, because a U-boat attempting to attack a ship doing 28–30 knots had a very very short time, if the U-boat was ever lucky enough to get into a firing position, to sight and fire torpedoes, and so these ships relied on their speed more than anything else. However, they were escorted by the destroyer part of the escort group for the first three or four days of their voyage out from the North of Ireland. It was extremely hardgoing for the destroyers because, as I think I mentioned previously, that these ships had been designed really for fleet work in the North Sea. The Atlantic was something very different and even in moderate westerly weather driving a destroyer at 28 knots into the sea is really a most painful experience for everybody on board.

I think it would be interesting to say something about the way we lived in these ships in the North Atlantic at that time in the war. We certainly never undressed, it would be quite impossible to dress if the ship suddenly had to go to action stations. You were expected to be at your action station within seconds of the alarm bells going, and we went to bed with all our clothes on except oilskins and sea boots which were kept very handy so that you could be out of your bunk, into your sea boots, on oilskins and up onto the bridge in well under a minute. Another factor was that the ships were very cold below decks. The wardroom was designed to be heated by a stove which had a chimney which went up above the X-gun and that of course had to be dismantled when the ship was at sea in wartime, so the stove couldn't be used. It was a delight in harbour but it was absolutely no use at sea. We had electric radiators but as the war progressed more and more new electronic equipment was fitted into the ship and the supply of power became very limited, so it was not possible, when at sea, to operate the radiators in the accommodation, with the result that the whole of the inside of the ship, including the living quarters for both officers and men, was cold and damp and really not very pleasant.

The ship had two mess decks at the forward end and the upper mess deck had no watertight doors to close it against following seas, with the result that if the ship was running before a heavy sea the sea could wash right into the mess deck, which was pretty miserable for the sailors. However, there were compensations, because the sailors slung their hammocks fairly high up and when the ship was subject to violent motion you were probably slightly better off in a hammock than you were in a bunk. The officers all had cabins; there was a cabin on the upper deck which was always known as the hen-house where the two most junior sub-lieutenants lived. I, fortunately, never had to suffer that accommodation, but it was pretty horrendous in bad weather: seas could wash in and if anyone was stupid enough to open the door they could invite a large part of the Atlantic Ocean in beside them. The rest of the officers all lived in the after end of the ship and the wardroom and the four cabins of the most senior officers were entered through the screen at the after end of the superstructure on which the X-gun was situated so that it was reasonably accessible. The more junior officers shared four cabins further aft and these four cabins had two very serious disadvantages. The first was that they were entered through a round hatch in the open deck. Getting into the accommodation was not too bad because one could wait in the shelter of the screen of the after superstructure until one thought that the sea conditions were propitious, then dash out, open the hatch, dash down into the hatch and shut it behind you before the next wave. Coming up from one's cabin to the deck was a slightly more difficult proposition because you had to rely on your ears and not your eyes to know when the quarter-deck, where this round hatch was situated, was reasonably clear of water, and you had to time the thing fairly carefully so that when the after end of the ship was well up in the air you opened the hatch, jumped out and ran into the shelter of the screen. Later on in *Keppel* we managed to persuade one of the dockyards where the ship was being refitted to cut a door through the sponson of Y-gun which separated the wardroom from the fore and after cabins and that enabled us to go from the fore and after cabins directly into the wardroom so that we could come up in the shelter of the after superstructure and avoid the difficulties that I have been describing. The second disadvantage was that the four after cabins were directly over the ship's propellers, so they were very noisy. In bad weather the propellers could come nearly out of the water. This made a terrible noise.

The problem for all the officers was getting from the after accommodation to the bridge to go on watch and getting back from the bridge to their cabin at the end of their watch period. In very bad weather a very taut wire was set up leading from the superstructure on which the bridge was situated to the superstructure on the after end of the ship. This wire carried a number of rope toggles and the way of getting along the deck was to grab hold of one these toggles, wait for the ship to be reasonably clear of water, then dash along the deck and hopefully get to the other end before the next wave. It was noticeable that people were always more anxious to get from the bridge to their accommodation than they were to go in the opposite direction. I remember on one occasion being slightly too anxious. I had come off watch, possibly the middle watch at four o'clock in the morning, and I was anxious to get to my accommodation and didn't time my passage along the main deck of the ship as carefully as I should have and I was caught by a tremendous wave and swept off the wire and through the guard rails of the ship. Fortunately, I managed to catch the guard rails on the way through, so I was left hanging outside the hull of the ship. The ship then took a very heavy roll in the opposite direction and I was able to scramble back on board and get one leg over the lower guard rail before the next wave had hit, and I was reasonably able to retain my position until I could scramble up and get hold of the wire again.

Bad weather had a tremendous effect on the ship's company generally; everything became so difficult—it was difficult to eat, difficult to sleep, and one had to lash oneself into one's bunk. In the cabins at the after end of the ship the propeller coming out of the water every so often made a tremendous noise and it was really very difficult, even for people like myself who have never had much trouble sleeping. It was also very tiring trying to walk anywhere, trying to stand up, moving about on the bridge on watch, conducting one's duties—and everybody got irritable. One compensation, of course, was that the U-boats couldn't operate successfully in that sort of weather so one really was fighting the elements and not the enemy a lot of the time, especially during the winter.

One of the problems that these ships suffered was that the condensers which condensed the steam exhausted from the turbines back into water suffered somewhat due to age. The condenser was simply a mass of tubes which the steam entered from the turbine. It was surrounded by sea water, but if there was any breakage in the tubes then the sea water got into the boiler feed and that could prove serious. It would knock one of the engines out of commission completely. This was a fairly common occurrence and the remedy was to find the leaking tube, which was not too difficult once the condenser was opened up, but that could not be done in violent weather, and it was common to seek shelter in one of the fjords of the Faroe Islands. Very often ships headed into the Faroes with this condenser trouble. I remember on one occasion after some atrocious weather we limped into a fjord in the Faroe Islands and a muster of the crew showed that one of the ordinary seamen was missing. It was presumed that he had been washed overboard and the First-Lieutenant went down to his cabin to write the painful letter to the young man's mother, when one of the other seamen came to say that the fellow had been mortally seasick and had crept into the hammock netting to sleep it off. Others, not seeing him, had piled their hammocks into the netting and he could neither get out nor make himself heard.

CHAPTER FIVE

The Atlantic Battle

By 1941 Londonderry had become the main base for the escorting forces for the Atlantic convoys. *Keppel* was mainly engaged as the leader of an escort group accompanying slow convoys across the Atlantic. Occasionally, however, we were sent down to the Mediterranean, which was a complete change of scene. Our job was to escort aircraft carriers to the vicinity of Malta where the carriers flew off their aircraft to help to defend that beleaguered island.

Londonderry was a pleasant place from which to operate because it seemed to be away from the war. Londonderry is situated some miles up the River Foyle from Loch Foyle and, coming in from our Atlantic convoys, it was very pleasant to sail up the River Foyle, almost parting the trees and seeing swans and all sorts of wildlife on the river. The people in Londonderry were very friendly and kind to us. It so happened that most of the social contacts that we made in Londonderry were Roman Catholic girls; they were WRENS and we met them through their duties in the operations room in the base. Even in those days one of the very interesting things about society in Northern Ireland was that there was no contact whatsoever between the Catholic population and the Protestant community (and I suppose Londonderry was a predominantly Catholic city). They were socially divided, they worked separately and the girls that we knew had no Protestant contacts whatsoever except through the Navy while they were serving as WRENS.

We were made honorary members of the Northern Counties Club, which was a fairly extreme Protestant organisation. It was a social club, and a very pleasant place to go. We used to spend quite a lot of time there but it was very interesting that the people one met in that club had no social contact across the religious divide either. They were Protestants, they worked with Protestants, they had their social life with Protestants, they knew there were a lot of Catholics around but they had no social contact with them whatsoever.

In *Keppel* a number of us had motorbikes and as soon as we got into harbour we used to get our motorbikes off the ship and drive off, very often across the border, and sometimes with girlfriends. The situation in the Irish Free State was that they seemed to have plenty of sugar and no tea whereas in the North of Ireland there seemed to be a reasonable amount of tea but no sugar, and we found that cross-border trading was very profitable. We used to take the girls across and barter with the people on the other side of the border and bring back whatever we could. Of course I mentioned previously that we did occasionally run down to the Azores to bunker and that enabled us to load up with bananas and pineapples which were absolutely unheard of in wartime and therefore excellent trading goods; one could get all sorts of things for pineapples and bananas on the other side of the border.

We, who had motorbikes, used to tow less fortunate members of the wardroom from *Keppel* on bicycles attached with ropes. I suppose it was perhaps not the safest way of travel but it was very efficient and it enabled those without motorbikes to get around the country, which was, incidentally, attractive country. The people on the other side of the border were most hospitable, and very often one would be invited into houses. I remember on one occasion we had stopped in a little village in Donegal somewhere and a lady came out and said, 'Would you like a cup of tea?' We thought this would be very nice indeed and went into her house, and I can remember being quite staggered because it was a small farmhouse and I was fascinated by the state of the range in the kitchen. It was absolutely red with rust, and I had been used to similar houses in Scotland where the ranges were always beautifully black leaded and the silver parts shining bright. The lady noticed my attention and she said 'I see you looking at my range. I cleaned it once and I hurt my back and I've never touched it since.' That really seemed to be typical of the attitude of the people in Donegal to their problems which is maybe no bad way to carry on.

On the first night in harbour in Londonderry, when we came back from an operation, we used to go to the Melville Hotel where they had a magnificent grill room, one of these old fashioned grills piled with glowing hot coals. One could have a wonderful mixed grill, and after wardroom food in *Keppel*, which was acceptable but not always terribly exciting, it was very pleasant for all of us to spend an evening at a round table served by a charming lady whose name escapes me now. She knew exactly what we wanted to eat, and she really used to pile the plates with this delicious mixed grill. It was a very pleasant way to spend an evening.

As the months went by, the battle of the Atlantic became more and more acute and our defences against U-boat attack were not very good. We had Asdics, i.e., underwater sonar which worked on high frequency sound. The ship had an oscillator which sent out a beam of high

35

frequency sound and the operator swung his beam over 5° intervals around the compass, and if he got an echo he reported it to the bridge and we investigated. However, U-boats almost always attacked on the surface, or at least trimmed down so that their conning towers were above the surface. This enabled them to proceed at a much higher speed than they could attain when they were fully submerged. The advent of radar greatly improved our ability to beat the U-boat threat. The first radar fitted to *Keppel* was rather primitive. It consisted of a very large aerial which we called a bedstead because it looked something like the springs of a bed. It was on the foremast and could not be directed. The aerial sent out radar beams all around the fore part of the ship and the radar operator had before him a cathode ray tube which displayed echoes which came from the starboard and port aerials. If these echoes were exactly similar in length then the echo was dead ahead. If on the other hand the starboard echo was much larger than the port then obviously the target was on the starboard bow. A reasonably competent operator could tell to within perhaps five degrees what the bearing of the target was. This was very helpful indeed, and it also made a very considerable difference to our station-keeping abilities on the convoy because *Keppel*, being the senior ship in the escort group, always took station ahead of the convoy, and this could be quite difficult because the convoy zigzagged in accordance with one pattern and *Keppel* zigzagged in accordance with another pattern. This was done to confuse any attacking U-boat, but it was quite difficult on a very dark night to zigzag ahead of a convoy, although we were only half a mile ahead. Sometimes it was hard to see if there were any ships there at all, and at the relief of a watch it was always necessary for the officers going off watch to be able to demonstrate that the convoy was still in sight, because otherwise the next watch refused to take over. There were occasions, though rare, when daylight came and there was no convoy in sight at all. Even our primitive radar improved these problems, as it was quite possible to judge exactly how far one was ahead of the convoy by radar range. Unfortunately, this heavy bedstead aerial was too much for *Keppel's* topmast, and running down to the Azores bucking into a head sea the wooden topmast found the strain too much and it broke just above the junction with the main foremast. The stays holding up the topmast were across the yard and the aerial was left swinging around violently; the man in the crow's nest was in a vulnerable situation. I was on the bridge at the time, so I called the Captain who said, 'Dickson, you've always rather fancied yourself as a seaman have you not?' and I said 'Yes, I have, Sir,' and he said, 'Right, you nip up the mast and clear away that wreckage.' The first thing I had to do was to get a rope around the aerial and I managed to secure it to stop it swinging about. I climbed up onto the yard and with a hammer and chisel cut through the steel stays and eventually succeeded in freeing the aerial, which then fell down the forward funnel of the destroyer, much to the chief engineer's disgust. However, this was not much of a problem, because the hot gases from the boilers meant the wood of the old foremast was just burnt away as was the metal.

In a way, it was a fortunate incident because it meant that instead of getting a new topmast and a new, type 2–8–5 'bedstead', we got a very much more accurate radar, the first of the 2–7 series: a 2–7–1. This meant an enormous improvement in our ability to determine targets by both bearing and range which is what radar is meant to do. The 2–7–1 was slightly limited in its application because the early sets of that type had wires going up to the aerial, and these wires wound around the pedestal on which the aerial was sited and eventually the operator had to wind the aerial back the other way in order to disentangle the wires. Another disadvantage was that it was sited in a steel hut which had to be placed on the bridge. The hut was rather heavy and it somewhat affected the motion of the ship. These destroyers were rather lively anyway but the addition of this radar at such a height on the bridge made the ship's motion even more violent than it had been before. However, we soon got used to radar and it improved our gunnery accuracy very substantially, because previously the only way one could determine the range was by optical range finders which were not very accurate and were very difficult to operate in bad weather. The radar gave extremely accurate range, and in fact when we did gunnery practice you could follow the shells on radar and see just how they were doing in respect to the target.

About this time the anti-submarine forces in Londonderry were expanded by American destroyers of 14–18 war vintage which had been given to Britain under arrangements made between Churchill and Roosevelt. They were not nearly as good as our 14–18 war destroyers, but they made a substantial addition to the number of ships operating from Londonderry. I've mentioned that our destroyers of the 14–18 war vintage were rather difficult ships in the North Atlantic in winter and I have to say that these American ships were even worse and some of those who sailed in them had a wet and miserable time. I suppose one of the advantages they had was that they had closed bridges; our bridge was open to the elements so that you got the full brunt of all weather conditions.

The Londonderry escort forces were also supplemented by coastguard cutters which had been acquired from America; these were excellent ships for the North Atlantic. They had, in fact, been built to operate in the high North Atlantic so they were more than able to stand up to all the weather we encountered.

An interesting thing worth noting is that a sub-lieutenant RNVR joined one of these coastguard cutters. He joined as Sub-Lieutenant Roberts and after a while letters arrived at the ship addressed to Lord Rothermere (I can't remember the exact title, but let's say Lord Rothermere, as it will do for the purpose) and Roberts took these letters, and it became obvious to everyone that although he called himself Sub-Lieutenant Roberts he was in fact Lord Rothermere. Everybody thought he was very decent was because he wasn't using his title and he was just behaving as an ordinary sub-lieutenant RNVR, and he was a very popular fellow around the base. After a while he hoisted a DSC ribbon and people asked him where he got his DSC. He said 'Well, I don't like to talk about it, it was a pretty nasty operation and I lost a lot of friends.' People once again talked about what a good fellow he was; not only was he Lord Rothermere but he had a DSC and was much too modest to say anything about it. In due time the coastguard cutter in which he was serving had a boiler clean and gained leave and this chap went to London where he and his girlfriend chose to stay at the Savoy Hotel and treated themselves fairly lavishly to anything that the Savoy Hotel had to offer. On the day when he had to leave and pay his bill he had nowhere near enough money to meet the bill so he decided that he would just sign and he used his title, Lord Rothermere. It just so happened that there was a lord of that title and the bill was referred to him. He was a crusty old gentleman who hadn't stayed at the Savoy with a girlfriend in recent memory and he was rather cross about it. It came to light that this chap was not Lord Rothermere, nor was he Sub-Lieutenant Roberts—in fact he was not even in the Navy. It is quite incredible, but in those days when one joined the ship, no one ever asked to see any documents. It was just accepted that the fellow was who he claimed to be, and as the pay documents very often took many many months to catch up, common practice was that when one joined a ship one was paid on a temporary basis until many months later when the pay documents arrived and the whole thing could be straightened out. This chap had obviously had friends who were serving in these ships and they had told him how things were done and he thought it would be a jolly good wheeze to do what he did. He went along to Moss Bros., bought himself a uniform, and off he went and joined one of the coastguard cutters. In due time, of course, he was court martialed and that was the end of that.

In June 1941 Commander Sheffield was relieved by Commander

Jackie Broome. Commander Sheffield went to the Admiralty and I believe that there he served as an advisor to the naval architects designing the new destroyers being built in the late 1940s. Commander Jackie Broome was a very well-known chap in the Navy; he was a submariner by service but much to his disgust he had been regarded as being too old to serve in submarines in the war. His first command was one of the V-class destroyers but he left her and joined *Keppel* as senior officer on the first escort group in June 1941. He was a very successful escort group Commander. It must be noted that some of the other escort groups had much greater success in killing U-boats, but Broome's success was in getting his convoys across the Atlantic by avoiding U-boat attack. He used all sorts of ploys to achieve this objective, and I must say I admired him very much. He did not spare himself at all when he was at sea and very often he would resort to strange tactics. He understood very well how the U-boats were likely to operate in any given circumstances. In the early part of the war U-boats attacked the convoys independently but the German Admiralty realised early on that substantial numbers of U-boats attacking a convoy simultaneously would be much more efficient, and what they did was to string their U-boats across the Atlantic. When one U-boat made contact with a convoy he would home a number of other U-boats onto him. Operating on the surface they could then keep ahead of the convoy until they were in a very good attacking formation and then they would attack, almost always at night, and on the surface, or trim down so that they could use their speed. It meant that they could operate with diesels instead of having to operate on battery power.

Keppel was helped in some way in meeting this particular type of attack by the fitting of HFDF (High Frequency Direction Finding) equipment which enabled us to listen to the U-boats and to understand what sort of U-boat force was mustering ahead and to take whatever action might be necessary in the given circumstances. Broome's expertise as a submarine commander over many years helped him enormously in understanding just what the U-boats could and could not do in any given circumstances and on more than one occasion he was able to arrange his escort in such a way that the U-boats who normally made first visual contact with the wing escorts found themselves with wing escorts that were quite far removed from the convoy, very much further than they expected, and very often their attack was to a large extent frustrated by such tactics.

However, he was not an easy man to serve under, and if there was an officer in whom he did not have absolute confidence he would make his life miserable, and on more than one occasion he drove people out of the ship by reducing them to a nervous state that just did not enable them to serve properly. He got them relieved and replaced by people he could trust and get along with. He made me his staff officer and one of the jobs that I had to do was to write reports of proceedings. Commander Broome brought his wife over to Londonderry and rented a flat in the city and as soon as the ship got into Londonderry after an operation he would nip ashore. In fact he very often brought the ship up the River Foyle in his blazer and flannels and as soon as the ship was tied up alongside he was off. I was then left with the task of going around the other ships of the groups and collating a report of proceedings, which he would sign and dispatch to Captain D, a Philip Ruck-Kean, who was in charge of the whole operation in Londonderry. One of the commanding officers of a flower class corvette in the group was a man called Nicholas Montserrat who became quite famous for writing a book called *The Cruel Sea*, and he was a very difficult chap to deal with in respect of this matter of the report of proceedings, because most of the commanding officers had great difficulty in managing a page of foolscap in their report, whereas Montserrat could manage many pages of foolscap giving his personal views and opinions of the tactical situation—he was an author of some note even in those days. But the reports of proceedings weren't really what it was all about; what it was all about was what happened in the Atlantic during operations and Broome realised this and he didn't really worry too much. All he wanted was for me to make a reasonable job of producing a whole report from the group and he would come on board perhaps an hour or half an hour before the ship was due to sail on the next operation, sign the report of proceedings of the previous operation and off it would go to Captain D. I don't know that Captain D ever really made very much of these reports of proceedings but they were a headache as far as I was concerned.

Sometimes the Atlantic duties were interrupted by Mediterranean convoys which were really very different to the Atlantic convoys in that the weather was obviously very much kinder, particularly in the summer, but the enemy activity was much greater. It was quite a good break from the Atlantic to go down and do a Mediterranean convoy, although they happened rarely. As I have said, we were mainly engaged on convoys to Malta, and on more than one occasion we had to take aircraft carriers to the area, with fighter aircraft which were then flown off the carriers and landed in Malta to reinforce the air defences of the island.

The Italians had a poor fighting reputation. The Italian navy had not covered itself with glory in the early part of the war, I think largely because the ships were so badly designed. The hearsay in the British Navy, which may or may not be accurate, was that Mussolini had instructed his naval architects to produce ships which carried bigger guns and were faster than the allied ships that he was likely to meet in the Mediterranean. He was very anxious to establish the Mediterranean as his *mare nostrum* and I understand that the received wisdom in the Royal Navy was that the naval architects had told Mussolini that these things were impossible and he said that he would get somebody else who could do it, so he eventually got naval architects who built ships to meet all his requirements. The difficulty was that they ran out of fuel after about 24 hours, so his navy really did not have much strength. However, there were some parts of the Italian operations in the Mediterranean which were extremely efficient and one of them was torpedo bombers. Another was their midget submarines and equivalents of E-boats. I never had to deal with either midget submarines or E-boats but we did have quite a lot of trouble with torpedo bombers, not specifically the *Keppel*, but the carriers that we were trying to get to Malta.

I remember on one occasion one of the carriers being sunk, and we managed to get into position and put scrambling nets over the side. We launched boats so that we picked up a number of survivors, many of whom were covered in fuel oil. In due time I went down to my cabin in the after end of the ship to find a young pilot officer, a fleet air arm chap in my bed, covered in fuel oil—which didn't please me very much. So I said, 'Where do you come from?' or rather, 'Where the hell do you come from?!' and he said, 'I come from Aberdeen.' So I said 'That's all right'. My servant helped me and we managed to get all the oily stuff off the bunk and put down some oilskins on which this chap could lie because we had no spare clothes for him and we were going to take him into Malta. Strangely enough that same fellow became a geologist in Shell and I met him many many years later in Borneo when we were both in the oilfield.

I have already said that our Captain, Commander Jackie Broome, was a very severe disciplinarian, and I remember a rather dreadful example of just how severe he could be. A medical officer had joined the ship, a man named Surgeon—Lieutenant McKendrick—he was a Scot. He had qualified and done his hospital time in Glasgow and he was obviously not a naval man. He had simply joined the Navy and been made a Surgeon-Lieutenant. RNVR and destroyers in those days always carried doctors. It was common practice that the medical officer did the ciphers, because ciphers were secret messages that had to be deciphered by a commissioned officer and the custom in the ship at that time was that watchkeeping was quite severe on the watchkeeping officers. All the executive officers of the ship were watchkeepers and they were either in three watches, or, if the conditions were fairly strained at the time, were on double watches, that is four hours on and four hours off. It was customary for the doctor, when ciphers arrived in the middle of the night, to decipher the messages and I remember I was on watch, it was a first watch—that is from eight o'clock at night until midnight. A cipher came in, maybe at about ten o'clock that night. I sent the bosun's mate to carry the messages to the doctor to have the cipher deciphered. In due time the bosun's mate arrived back on the bridge and said: 'The Medical Officer is sorry, Sir, but he can't decipher the message'.

By this time Jackie Broome had arrived on the bridge. At sea he always wore the same rig: he had a pair of airforce boots, grey flannel trousers, two very heavy jerseys—the top one was quite commonly a natural sheep's wool jersey which more or less shed water—and around his neck he wound a long length of chamois leather which shed the water very well. The ship by this time was taking a fair bit of spray and Broome, hunched in his chair, heard the bosun's mate report and was not too pleased at this. So he said to the bosun's mate, 'You go down and tell the Doctor that the Captain orders him to do the cipher'. So off went the bosun's mate once again and arrived back on the bridge shortly afterwards and said, 'The Doctor sends his compliments to the Captain but says that he still can't do the cipher because it is against the Geneva Convention'. At this Commander Broome really lost his rag. He always kept a 45 revolver in his sea cabin hanging beside his bunk and he appeared back on the bridge brandishing this revolver and said to the bosun's mate, 'Tell the doctor that I require his presence on the bridge immediately.' I was absolutely terrified, I didn't know what was going to happen next, because Broome had on more than one occasion mentioned his admiration of a British submarine commander who had shot one of his crew on the conning tower of his submarine in the Dardanelles in the 14–18 war for disobedience of orders. In due time the Doctor arrived on the bridge in his Moss Bros. uniform, and just as he appeared the ship nosedived into a pretty heavy head sea and the whole bridge was covered in spray. This was perhaps a very fortunate occurrence because the Doctor was absolutely soaked. Broome turned round and he said, 'Medical Officer, I don't like you. I don't like people who don't obey orders and I was thinking seriously about bloody well shooting you but I've thought of a better idea. I want you to stay where you are on the bridge,' and with that he disappeared down his ladder into his sea cabin. Poor old McKendrick was soon in a sorry state. The ship was washing down all the time with very heavy spray and the doctor said to me, 'I'd better go down and get some waterproof clothing.' I said, 'It is more than your life's worth to leave the bridge. You stay where you are and you stay as you are.' So he did, and about 20 minutes later, by which time the poor old Doctor was absolutely soaked to the skin and bitterly cold, Broome appeared on the bridge. 'Doctor,' he said, 'You must be cold and wet', and the Doctor said that indeed he was. 'Go down then, and get some sleep', Broome said, and so off the doctor went thinking that at last all his troubles were over. About 20 minutes later, just having allowed enough time for the Doctor to get into his bunk and probably asleep, the Captain sent the bosun's mate down with the orders, 'Tell the Medical Officer that I want him on the bridge.' This time Surgeon-Lieutenant McKendrick appeared on the bridge with sou'wester, oilskins, sea boots—everything he could think of. Broome said to him, 'Doctor, you and I can go on like this for ever if you so wish.' The Doctor could see by this time that he was on an absolute loser so he said, 'All right sir, I'll do the ciphers', and that was the end of that.

Commander Broome had two other ways of dealing with officers who behaved in a way that didn't entirely meet with his approval, and one was to place them under open arrest. Two or three of the officers on the ship were under open arrest, which meant they had to stay in their cabins, which was unpleasant for them but equally unpleasant for their colleagues who had to cover for the watch-keeping duties which were lost due to the absence of people under open arrest. The other punishment which he commonly inflicted was to ask people to give their reasons in writing why they had done some act which had displeased him. It was quite a difficult punishment to satisfy because one had to anticipate what the most severe aspect of his displeasure was and then try and accommodate it in writing the best way one could. If one got it wrong then it simply infuriated the Captain even further. He was really a very harsh disciplinarian and a very difficult man to serve, but as I have said he was an extremely efficient escort group Commander and he was also an extremely good ship handler and in the Navy ship handling was one of the attributes of a Captain that was very much admired by his officers. I can remember on more than one occasion being very impressed with the way in which Jackie Broome could handle his destroyer. In the Atlantic we had a ship very severely damaged. I can't remember whether it was by aircraft or by U-boat, but the ship was going to sink and Broome put his destroyer almost alongside and people were able to scramble from the sinking merchant ship onto the destroyer. It was a very fine piece of ship handling.

I can however remember one rather hairy moment with Broome. We had gone out with the destroyers of the group, as was our custom, to escort one of the high-speed liners. It happened to be *Queen Mary*. We were due to rendezvous with the *Queen*, she steaming up the Irish Channel at high speed, at the northern end of the Irish Channel. The destroyers were spread to form an escort turning ahead of the *Queen* when she was sighted. Visibility was not very good and I can remember being very nervous about our steaming south at such a high speed knowing that the *Queen* was steaming north at an even higher speed. We sighted the *Queen* at fairly close distance in very poor visibility and had to turn the destroyers through 180 degrees. It was not a very comfortable situation. Previously the *Queen* had cut a C-class cruiser, HMS *Curacao*, in half, doing exactly the same thing, and I can remember we just got round onto the same course as the *Queen* steaming north, and I could see quite clearly the faces of the chaps standing on the decks of the *Queen Mary*. We got a signal from the *Queen Mary*: 'Very impressive but pretty damn frightening.'

Another fascinating thing I remember about this time was that we received a signal to the effect that the lighthouse keeper at the Mull of Kintyre had reported that a boat from his station had been stolen. The powers that be assumed that this had been stolen by a German spy and *Keppel* was ordered to see if we could catch this fellow. Strangely enough, because looking for a small boat in the north part of the Irish Channel was not really an easy task, we were very lucky. We ran right across this fellow busy in his small boat, and we came alongside him and asked if he wanted any assistance. He said he did, so we pulled him aboard and he asked in faultless English whether we could help him because he was on his way to Ireland. The only thing he had in his possession was a copy of *Mein Kampf*. In due time the German spy was turned over to the army and I imagine that he would have been shot, poor chap.

In the early part of 1942 the battle of the Atlantic was assuming pretty terrible proportions. There were reckoned to be somewhere around 150 U-boats operating in the Atlantic in March of 1942 and they were taking a great toll of the various convoys, although one of the things that made me admire Commander Broome very much was that we lost very few ships. It was customary to regard the success of the various escort groups by the number of U-boats they sank. On this Commander Broome's First Escort Group did not do very well. In fact, we only sank one U-boat during his command. However, we lost fewer ships than all the other groups and to a great extent this was due to Broome's ability to outmanoeuvre the U-boat packs.

44

By far our greatest threat was the U-boat, but there were also Focke-wulf bombers. They were converted airliners which the Germans used for reconnaissance. The Focke-wulfs flew far out into the Atlantic to find convoys and give positions to the U-boat packs. They carried bombs and once they had reached the limit of their endurance they would attack convoys on their way back to base. I remember on one occasion a Focke-wulf bombed and sank a fine ship in one of our convoys and then flew almost directly over *Keppel*. We had a Vickers 303 machine gun on the wing of the bridge—it wasn't really much better than a pea shooter but it was something. I remember diving for this machine gun and the Yeoman of the Signals who was on the bridge at the same time also dived for the gun, with the result that I got there first and pressed the firing trigger. Then the Yeoman arrived and knocked me off balance. All we did was put a line of bullet holes through the forward funnel which was not exactly useful.

CHAPTER SIX

The Arctic

I suppose it must have been fairly early in June 1942 that we in *Keppel* learned that we were going to go from Londonderry up to Iceland to escort a convoy to Murmansk. I must say that we knew fairly well through Admiralty intelligence reports how the Arctic convoys had been faring, and the thought of taking a convoy to Murmansk in the height of summer was most unappealing. However, in those days one did what one was told to do. We knew Iceland fairly well because we used to fuel regularly in Val fjord which lay to the west of Reykjavik. We had always found Iceland a rather forbidding place, and certainly the south of that country is subject to typical Atlantic weather. One thinks of Iceland as being an ice-covered island; it is, in fact, not at all. The climate is not dissimilar to the climate of Orkney or Shetland. It is subject to the depressions of the North Atlantic sweeping from west to east for most of the winter. I suppose it may be marginally colder, but it is certainly not an ice-covered island.

Our first port of call on the north of Iceland was Akureyri. I found the north coast of Iceland much more attractive than the south coast. Akureyri is a quite beautiful little town. It is entered through a long fjord which is quite difficult to navigate, particularly in fog, and we seemed to get a lot of fog at this time, but the township of Akureyri itself was most attractive. The houses were all painted in pastel shades of yellow, blue and pink and it really was quite a delightful little place. We went ashore and there was a swimming pool which the local people told us was heated with hot water from the hot springs. This may have been so, but we were foolish enough to dive into this swimming pool, and if it was heated by the hot springs it wasn't heated very much. It was bitterly cold! However, the people in the north of Iceland seemed to be much more friendly than the people that we had encountered in Reykjavik.

The assembly point in Iceland for the convoy PQ17 was Seidisfjord. At Seidisfjord we met up with the heavy escort for PQ17 which consisted of four eight-inch cruisers. The squadron being commanded by Vice-Admiral Hamilton, who had been my Captain in HMS *Delhi*, consisted of his flagship *London*, the *Norfolk*—another British eight-inch cruiser—and two modern American eight-inch cruisers, *Wichita* and

Tuscaloosa. There were a number of conferences in Seidisfjord about the running of the convoy, and I was involved in these since I was Staff Officer to Jackie Broome who was to command the escort. The American Staff Officer to the senior Captain of the two American eight-inch cruisers was Douglas Fairbanks Jnr, and I remember coming back from one of these conferences in a launch with Fairbanks and listening to him chatting to one of the other American Officers. The point that he was making was that he was surprised at the ancient British ships that had been assembled to conduct this convoy to Russia.

Being a fairly junior man in the Navy I really don't know all of the logic behind this dispatch of a convoy to Russia in the high summer, but my own interpretation of the situation is that the meeting between the Heads of States which had just taken place was at a time when the British were under great pressure with the Americans to open the second front in Europe by the Russians, who were suffering dreadful casualties on their front. I am sure that the Americans and the British wanted to do everything they possibly could to meet the Russians' desperate need for help and my understanding was that it was agreed that the southern–northern supply routes would be kept open and as much war supplies as possible would be made available to Russian forces.

I imagine there were no problems as far as the southern supply route through the Persian Gulf was concerned, but when the Naval Command were instructed to continue supply to north Russia by the Arctic convoy route throughout the summer I imagine that the Admiralty's response may well have been that this was not feasible. The convoys would have to pass very close to the heavily staffed air bases in northern Norway and it would have been quite impossible to provide either adequate anti-aircraft cover or indeed heavy surface cover. It was known that the *Tirpitz* and a number of other heavy ships were in Norway ready to intercept convoys on the Russian route, and of course the thought of risking an aircraft carrier to provide adequate air cover against air attacks was from the Admiralty's point of view unthinkable. Of course, these are only my own views, as I could not possibly know the underlying thinking of the high command of the Navy on these matters. As far as we were concerned, assembling in Seidisfjord, we knew that the intent was that the whole of the Home fleet under the command of Admiral Tovey would put to sea and pretend to be a convoy. The fleet would then take a route far to the south of the one proposed for our PQ17 hoping that they might draw the enemy surface forces. This did not work at all because the German air reconnaissance all over the high part of the North Sea and up into the Arctic was extremely efficient and they knew exactly what was going on. What I do know is that Admiral Hamilton was under instruction to avoid placing his ships in a position of danger, except where it was absolutely necessary to protect the convoy. Broome had a conference with the escort group commanders at which he made it clear that his intent was that if the convoy were to be attacked by enemy surface ships, the destroyers carrying torpedoes would form into a striking force under the code word 'strike' which would be given on VHF radio. The plan was that they were to form on him in *Keppel* and then proceed at high speed to make a torpedo attack on the enemy surface forces. As far as defence against aircraft was concerned the convoy included two heavily armed ships—the *Posarica* and the *Palomares*—both of which had a considerable armament of twin four-inch high-angle guns, but in my experience naval gunnery has never been a successful way of dealing with substantial air attack. The rest of the escort of the convoy had very dubious anti-aircraft gunnery defence. We had one merchant ship with a catapult aircraft on the fore end of the ship. These catapult aircraft were piloted by very brave chaps, because once they had been shot off on their catapults there was no way they could ever land anywhere, and they had to parachute down into the sea and hope that they could be picked up before they froze to death, which was most unlikely.

In the event, having gone through all the discussions and planning sessions in Seidisfjord, the convoy eventually set sail and proceeded on its way to Murmansk. It was not very long before we suffered the first air attack, and I remember that our sailors in *Keppel* had been very interested in the fact that one of the Russian ships in the convoy was manned partially by women. This Russian ship was one of the first ships to be hit by an aircraft-carried torpedo in the first of the air attacks. She was lying with a bit of a list astern of the convoy after the attack and *Keppel* swept round, much to the interest of the crew, to see how this ship was faring and whether she could get back on station in the convoy or not. Broome took his ship close up alongside the Russian and many of *Keppel's* crew appeared on deck to see how these Russian ladies were behaving. They were a really astonishing looking lot of people. I remember looking through my binoculars and seeing these Russian ladies with their arms all tattooed and black straggly hair. They really were most unattractive. However, they were very tough and they had got their boats ready for lowering and the ship appeared not too badly damaged, so that by the time we got alongside them they were making quite reasonable speed and they eventually caught up with the convoy again.

Broadly speaking, Admiral Hamilton's idea was, in consultation with

Broome who had ultimate responsibility for the convoy's safety, to get the convoy as far north as possible with the aim of getting it as far as possible away from the aircraft flying from the air bases in the north of Norway. To this end his cruiser lowered a Walrus aircraft which flew up and determined where the edge of the Arctic ice was. It was my first experience of the high Arctic and one of the things that struck me was how absolutely beautiful it was. One thinks of ice as being white and icebergs as being lumps of white ice floating around in the sea. Midsummer in the Arctic is in fact a brilliantly coloured period. The ice can be anything from the blue of the sea, though green to white, and the sea can be an absolutely brilliant azure blue dazzling in the sunlight. At the same time, you can suddenly run into freezing fog. It was very interesting, because when the ship entered the freezing fog everything froze immediately, so the guns' crews had to keep the guns training and elevating all the time to prevent them from freezing. Despite the fact that it was high summer it could be intensely cold. There was of course no night, as the sun never went below the horizon. In the fog, the temperature went down well below zero and some extraordinary things would happen. For example, you could be having a cup of cocoa, which was the watch keeper's great saviour against cold and hunger on the bridge, and it would suddenly freeze in the cup.

As the convoy got further east the aircraft attacks became more and more regular. We had a German Blohm-voss 138 aircraft, which was a flying boat, in contact with the convoy most of the time signalling our position, course and speed to those back in the Norwegian airbases so there was absolutely no possibility of any disguise for the convoy. We just had to suffer wave after wave of air attack. This meant that sleep was absolutely impossible, and the ship's company became increasingly dispirited.

Fear is a strange thing, and I remember in the general naval teaching one of the instructions was that everyone should use fear to assist them in what they had to do, and I think there is a lot of sense in that. You can, I believe, use fear intelligently and there need not be any connection between fear and panic. In circumstances where one is fairly convinced one is not going to make it, the intent is to sell your life as dearly as possible and this was the mood in the ship.

I don't remember how many days we suffered almost 24-hour air attack, but whenever the fog cleared an air attack could be expected. At about the beginning of July we were subjected to our old friend the U-boat as well as air attacks. By this time we had almost run out of high-angle ammunition. I remember on one occasion coming off watch in fairly thick fog. As I've said, there were these diesel driven Blohm-voss

138 aircraft constantly in touch with the convoy, and obviously they were as nonplussed in fog as we were. On the starboard sponson just below the bridge we had single oerlikon guns, and I remember hearing one of these diesel driven Blohm-voss 138 coming towards the ship. So I waited beside the oerlikon gun with the gun at the ready and this German aircraft came out of the fog and flew right over the top of the ship. I understand that these aircraft are fairly heavily protected underneath the important parts of the aircraft, but I managed to get off a burst of oerlikon gunfire and I could see the gun shells bursting on the bottom of the flying boat. It never brought the aircraft down but I hope he had a nasty time when he landed in the sea somewhere in Norway. Aircraft attacks were really very fierce indeed and on many occasions I remember *Keppel* having to execute some fairly violent manoeuvres to avoid torpedoes from the Hienkel 115 torpedo attack plane.

Then, one day, the real horror happened. A signal arrived, perhaps on 3 July, from the Admiralty, to the effect that the battleship *Tirpitz*, an eight-inch cruiser—I think the *Hipper*—and four Narvik class destroyers had left Norway to intercept the convoy. Again I speak with only my own understanding of the situation, but I believe Admiral Hamilton had been instructed not to proceed too far to the east of the convoy, because the Admiralty were desperately anxious not to lose any more cruisers on the Arctic route to Russia, since they had already lost quite a few. However, Hamilton, being the man he was, probably disobeyed his orders, and he was rather further east than he should have been, placing himself as he thought between the possible enemy attacking ships and the convoy. There were also two British submarines with the convoy. They were supposed to be deployed ahead of the convoy in the direction from which enemy ships would be expected to attack. One amusing anecdote is that the senior officer of the two submarines moving out into the appropriate position sent a signal to Broome which was, 'In the event of attack by enemy surface forces I intend to remain on the surface', to which Broome replied, 'So do I.'

On 4 July came a signal from the Admiralty to the effect that the convoy PQ17 was to scatter. Broome reasonably assumed that this meant the enemy surface forces were fairly close to the convoy. He went alongside the Commodore of the convoy ship and told him that he had received this message that it was going to be a bloody business. He suggested that the convoy ships proceed independently as far north into the ice as they possibly could to avoid the attention of the German aircraft while he formed up the destroyers for an attack on the German forces, and he made his codeword 'strike'.

The destroyers detached themselves from the convoy and formed up on *Keppel* and the destroyer force proceeded eastwards hoping, or rather fearing, to meet the enemy surface forces. It may seem strange, but this was almost a relief. Up until that time I think the whole ship's company were not too confident in their future. However, once this signal came and it was appreciated that the destroyer force was going off to attack an infinitely superior German force, there was a mood of relief in the ship. Everyone then knew, or thought they knew, that this was the end of the road. Everyone thought the outcome was absolutely inevitable, and we were entirely resigned to do the best we could, but it wasn't going to be very good.

I remember the valiant gunner T struggling with his torpedoes because the torpedoes kept freezing in the tubes and it would have been the ultimate horror if we had got into an attacking position on the German ships and found that our torpedoes were stuck in the tubes. So there we were, this gallant band of mostly fairly elderly destroyers, racing towards the presumed oncoming, and by far superior, German heavy ships. I can remember very well looking through my binoculars on the bridge and seeing the tops of ships appear on the horizon. It was a beautiful clear day, absolutely 100% visibility and I remember thinking, 'That's it—now we know we've really had it'. As the fighting tops rose up above the horizon we realised it was not the Germans, but Hamilton, who had disobeyed his orders and proceeded far to the east of where he was supposed to be. He then made a signal to the Admiralty declaring his position because the Admiralty had made it clear that they wished to take charge of the operation. Having disclosed his position he was instructed to retire at high speed to the west. So instead of meeting the Germans we met the British and American cruisers. By this time, the aircraft were busy attacking the convoy, and they left the escorts and the cruiser alone. So, before we knew where we were, we were closing the cruiser force at a speed of something like 50 knots. Broome sent a signal to Admiral Hamilton, 'What are my instructions?' Hamilton's reply was, 'Join me.' After that there was a considerable collapse of morale in the ship. I don't suppose we could have done anything other than what had been done, but the naval escort's business is to look after a convoy, do or die, and many fine people had done just that. And here we were: we had done what we were told, we had scattered the convoy and then we had gone off to seek the enemy and found no enemy. That was why there was a collapse of morale in the ship.

Looking back on it I really can't see what we could have done differently. Much later in life Broome was subjected to a vitriolic account

51

of the whole business of PQ17, in a book written by a man named David Irving. Broome sued this man and I was asked to be a witness in his action against the author. I had a number of lunches with Broome and some of his naval friends, and it became obvious to me then that our beliefs about the convoy were at variance. Broome, as far as I can understand, believed that if the Admiralty hadn't sent this signal to the convoy to scatter he could have got the convoy to Murmansk. We had, in fact as I have previously mentioned, run out of high-angle ammunition; the ship had been in action for something like 48 hours continuously and we were getting nearer, not further, from the enemy attacking air bases. By that time we had run into fairly heavy U-boat attack and, quite frankly, I don't think that, had the convoy not been scattered, the results would have been substantially different.

Captain Broome, as he then was, won his action against David Irving. Strangely enough, the court case, in the High Court in London was disrupted by the Welsh Language Society which had nothing to do with it; but that happened before I was due to appear on Broome's behalf. It was obvious by that time that the judge had reached a conclusion, and that David Irving's book had in fact been an unfounded attack on the escort command. Captain Broome's claim for damages was justified and he was awarded £40,000. I have to say I still held my own view—and in discussion with Broome I made my views quite clear—whilst I understood well enough Broome's wish to clear his name against a scurrilous attack by this author, PQ17 had been a dreadful disaster, and a large number of people had lost their lives. It seemed to me that these people's relatives would follow the proceedings in court, which would bring back memories, and do very little good other than to clear Broome's name. His name stood well in naval circles; everybody knew that the disaster that had befallen the Russian convoy was certainly not his fault, and I could see no great advantage in his obtaining damages against this man. However, I was unable to convince Broome, who went ahead with the action and, as I say, was awarded damages to the sum of £40,000. I remember, as Commander Broome's Staff Officer, attending the conference prior to the departure of the next convoy, that there was a heated exchange between Broome and some American chaps in the conference about what had gone on in PQ17. The Americans seemed to think that Broome was culpable for the loss of the convoy.

On return from the Arctic, *Keppel* went back to Scapa Flow and Broome had to attend discussions with the Commander in Chief of the whole fleet, Admiral Tovey, about what had gone on with PQ17, and eventually, after evidence had been taken, *Keppel* returned to

Londonderry and we imagined that we would go back to convoy escort duty in the North Atlantic. However, that was not to be the case. Our next job was to go down to the Mediterranean and escort a convoy to Malta—Operation Pedestal.

The only similarity between Operation Pedestal and PQ17 was that both convoys suffered very heavy air attack, but the conditions in the Mediterranean were a lot more pleasant than the Arctic. It was a summer operation, of course; the weather was warm—instead of wearing heavy arctic clothes we were in shirts and shorts—and sometimes not even shirts. Another important difference was that in the Mediterranean there was, of course, a very considerable number of hours of darkness which we hadn't had in the Arctic. Therefore, the ship was able to return to watchkeeping—I think that the ship remained at action stations throughout the daylight hours but during the hours of darkness we could go into a cruising watchkeeping situation and it did mean that the ship's company could get a fair amount of sleep. In addition, whereas PQ17 had always been threatened by the possible attack of very heavy German surface forces, it was thought to be unlikely that Operation Pedestal would be similarly threatened. The Italian heavy ships had not made much attempt to attack the convoys to Malta and it was thought most unlikely that they would try to attack the forces supporting the convoy Operation Pedestal.

After the Malta convoy, the Admiralty decided that *Keppel* should be converted to a long range escort ship and the ship proceeded from Gibraltar into the Thames to Green and Silley Weir's docks for this conversion, which was going to involve taking out one of the ship's boilers. The ship had four boilers, to be reduced to three, which would give her much longer range, because the boiler would be replaced by additional fuel tanks. Also her anti-submarine equipment was going to be substantially increased, and it was a fairly long operation. The result of this was that the ship was going to be paid off and all the officers would disband and go to other ships.

On arrival in the Thames the ship was visited by the First Lord of the Admiralty, Mr A.V. Alexander. I'm not really sure to this day what the purpose of his visit was. Presumably it was to some extent an exercise to try to improve the morale of a rather dispirited ship after the operation PQ17. I remember that the ship's company was assembled on the quarter deck and addressed by this distinguished politician. I don't remember what he said, and it didn't seem to me that there was very much purpose in what he said. No doubt his intentions were entirely honourable.

CHAPTER SEVEN

H.M.S. Relentless

Like all the rest of the ship's company, I went on leave, and my next appointment was to join a new fleet destroyer, building in John Brown's yard in the Clyde. A flotilla of eight ships was being built at that time, and all had names beginning with 'R'—my ship was called *Relentless*.

It was very interesting being involved in John Brown's, and we used to lunch in the senior executive messroom in the yard where there was much talk about the building of the *Queens* which these chaps had been involved in. The food served in the messroom in John Brown's was certainly very much better than in any other restaurant in the country at that time, I would imagine.

There was a great deal to learn about the ship. She was launched by the wife of a director of Firth Brown, the steel people. Presumably, there was a connection between Firth Brown's and John Brown's of Clydebank—I don't know what the connection was. This good lady in due time launched the ship.

The officers spent much of their time trying to understand the fighting capabilities of this new ship. She was very different from *Keppel*—although her main armament of 4.7 guns was similar in size it was very different in technology. Whereas *Keppel*'s guns had been breech loaders, *Relentless* had semi-automatic 4.7's with a very considerable high-angle capability and the fire control arrangements for the guns in *Relentless* were streets ahead of what had been my experience in *Keppel*. She had an Admiralty fire control clock, which was a very sophisticated piece of equipment, and the anti-aircraft control arrangements were also very complicated and far in advance of what I had been used to. I found it extraordinary that although this was wartime and these ships were desperately needed, the behaviour of the fellows who were fitting out the ship was not such as one would think would be appropriate to trying to get the ship into good order as quickly as possible. I would come across fellows in the ship playing cards, drinking tea and doing all sorts of things other than getting on with the business of fitting the ship out.

However, eventually the ship was finished—I think it must have been about November 1942. The first business, of course, was to run the vessel through her trials before acceptance from the building yard. This was all done in the Clyde and the ship was then manned, primarily by people from the builder's yard, whose concern it was to satisfy the Navy that she would perform in accordance with the specification for her class.

In due time the trials were completed, the red ensign was pulled down and the white ensign hoisted. This meant the ship was in full commission. It was quite extraordinary how different the ship's company in *Relentless* were from the ship's company of *Keppel*. *Keppel* had been manned almost entirely by reservists, who were men who had served 12 years in the Navy. A number of them had come out, and done all sorts of other things and had been recalled to the colours, and both the able seamen and the petty officers were very experienced destroyer people. *Relentless*, on the other hand, was manned almost entirely by people who had never been to sea before—certainly as far as the seamen were concerned—the petty officers obviously had, but the seamen were very young, very raw and very inexperienced, and it made a great difference to the way in which the ship had to be run. It was certainly dawning on me that the problem in a new ship like *Relentless* was not being able to 'fight the ship', but for the sailors to be able to live in the ship, because as soon as they went to sea everybody was seasick. It was absolutely appalling. The way in which the mess decks were fed in destroyers was that each mess decided what their menu for the day was going to be, the main meal being in the middle of the day. Each man shared responsibility on a rota basis for making up the meal and taking it along to the galley. There was a routine pipe, 'cooks to the galley' and a man from each mess took his prepared food along to the galley where the cook cooked it. This, of course, didn't work at all well when the chaps were being violently seasick.

After commissioning in the Clyde we were sent up to Tobermory where there was a working up base run by a commodore called Stevenson, always known as Monkey Stevenson. He had been running this base for some time, preparing corvettes and frigates for service in the North Atlantic. We were the first fleet ship to be sent to his base. I think it was a good idea to be sent there because, as I have said, one of the problems was to try to get the ship to work so that people could be fed and live reasonably on the ship, and the working up arrangements played a part in this. When *Relentless* arrived at Tobermory I am quite sure that this Commodore Stevenson thought to himself, 'Well now, I'll show these fleet boys a thing or two.' Certainly, the officers in fleet destroyers considered themselves to be a cut above those serving in corvettes and frigates.

Shortly after arrival in Tobermory, the ship was lying at a buoy out in the middle of the harbour. One of the experienced petty officers in the ship, the gunner's mate, had had his house bombed in Portsmouth and the poor chap had been unable to sleep. He had come out onto the fo'c'sle of the destroyer at about two o'clock in the morning, and he heard the boat's falls running in the guardship, which was Commodore Stevenson's ship, and he realised that something was afoot. Something was indeed afoot. Commodore Stevenson had sent a boat over to try to steal *Relentless*'s log which, if he managed to do it, would have meant that the ship was not being properly guarded during the midnight hours. The gunner's mate had this all well under control and by the time the boat from the guardship arrived alongside *Relentless* he had hoses rigged. The idea was that these chaps from the boat were going to swarm up the ship's anchor cable which was attached to a buoy; they had a terrible time because the hoses were put on and the boat was given a thorough soaking and they retired back to the guardship in complete disorder. Stevenson was quite impressed with all this—he thought that it was a good show. I'm not sure that his boarding crew did.

Another amusing incident was when the Commodore himself decided to visit the ship. He came on board and as soon as he got up to the top of the gangway he threw his hat onto the deck and said, 'That's an incendiary bomb', and the Quartermaster, with great presence of mind, kicked his cap over the side into the water. Once again the old boy thought this was quite good, and he was quite happy to have his launch go round and pick up his sodden cap which was floating on the water.

Every day the ship had to go out to exercise areas, and we did full calibre shoots exercising the 4.7 guns and also sub-calibre shoots. Sub-calibre shoots were quite interesting: a small gun was put inside the 4.7 guns, to save on the cost of full-scale ammunition, and the whole gunnery control arrangements could be scaled down to take account of the fact that instead of firing a 4.7 shell we were firing a very small shell, not much bigger than a 20-mm oerlikon gun shell. These exercises involved the whole ship's company for most of the day, and the practice was that the ship used to leave Tobermory—we were in winter darkness of course—in time to arrive in the exercise area at first light. Then the ship would be exercised all through the day on either gunnery practice or anti-submarine. One of the old British submarines used to come up from the Clyde and exercise us in submarine detection. We also had anti-aircraft firing exercises. These were really of no use because we used to exercise the anti-aircraft guns against targets towed by very slow-flying aircraft, which had very little bearing on the much more sophisticated German aircraft that we were likely to meet later on, when the ship was fully commissioned. We stayed on the exercise area doing these things until dark, and then made our way back to Tobermory. This was a fairly tiring and arduous business for everyone on board the ship.

One Sunday morning, I remember, after the ship had done much of the working-up programme arranged for us, Stevenson had decided that it would be a good idea to have a competitive general drill between *Relentless* and another new ship. This ship, the *Wild Swan*, was an anti-aircraft sloop which had just been delivered from the shipbuilding yard. She was a beautiful new ship, armed with highly sophisticated twin four-inch guns with a very sophisticated anti-aircraft control system.

The Captain of *Relentless*, one Lieutenant Commander Robert Augustus Fell, was a very religious chap, and he was insistent that the ship should go to church parade every Sunday morning. He was conducting his service, as was his wont, on the quarterdeck of *Relentless*, with the church pennant flying at the yardarm when the Quartermaster came running around the after end screen to tell the Captain that something terrible was happening.

The Captain did not want to be disturbed in the middle of his church service, but the Quartermaster insisted, and eventually it became clear that a very serious problem had developed. The intention of the general drill was that the *Wild Swan* was to slip her cables from the buoy and get underway to come alongside *Relentless*. Stevenson was going to come on board; the plan was that he was going to have envelopes that had to be opened: the instruction to each ship would be to do something very silly: for example, to change the port whaler onto the starboard davits and the starboard whaler onto the port davit and things like that. There was to be stopwatch timing to see which ship achieved this rather stupid exercise in the shortest time. But the Quartermaster's news was that the *Wild Swan* was drifting across the harbour in the direction of the rocks lying on the other side of the bay from the town of Tobermory. Apparently, there had been a complete failure of communication in the ship and the engine room hadn't been told to get steam up, so all the deck crew appeared and the ship was slipped from her moorings. In those days destroyers disconnected their anchors when going to a buoy and secured the anchor cable chain to the buoy. So the ship slipped the anchor cables from the buoy and was hanging on the buoy on a wire; then she let go the wire. The Captain on the bridge rang his instructions to the engine room for whatever he wanted to do in the way of manoeuvering the ship, and found to his absolute horror that they were without steam. Of course, the cables had been disconnected from the anchors to attach to the buoy so there was no way that the ship could anchor. In a fairly light breeze they were just slowly drifting across the harbour towards the rocks.

Commodore Stevenson was on his way out in his barge to superintend his Sunday morning general drill, when he realised things were going very badly wrong. He came alongside *Relentless* and said, 'What are you going to do?' Well, the plan had been that *Relentless* was going to stay on her buoy, so we had no main steam either and quite obviously there was nothing that we could do and the Captain said, much to Stevenson's disgust, 'All I can suggest, Sir, is that we assist in the preparation of hot dinners for the *Wild Swan*, if that would be of any help.' I have to say this did not amuse Commodore Stevenson at all. The dreadful outcome was that *Wild Swan* did drift right across the harbour and went ashore on the rocks on the other side of Tobermory bay on a falling tide. So, there was this beautiful brand new ship, straight out of the builder's yard, lying hard aground a very nasty rocky bottom. There was very serious damage to the ship. However, on the next high tide it was possible to float her off, and she made her way back down to the yard at which she had been built. There she was dry docked for the necessary repairs.

Relentless then went up to Scapa Flow to join the home fleet, where we had perhaps a more sophisticated but no less arduous working-up programme to undertake. Scapa Flow was never my favourite place during the war. I remember one destroyer captain—I think it might well have been Commander Broome—said that if a man could take his ship into Scapa Flow, get her bunkered, get his mails and provisions and get out again without any mishap he had nothing at all to fear from the enemy.

Relentless's stay in Scapa Flow was absolutely horrendous. I mentioned that we had exercised our gunnery fairly extensively from the working-out base at Tobermory, but in Scapa Flow we had to exercise our torpedo firing. *Relentless* was fitted with quite sophisticated modern eight torpedoes in two lots of four tubes, and the control system was much better than I had been used to in *Keppel*. Our first torpedo firing exercise was against a target ship, a Greek destroyer called the *Adrias*. In due time we found the *Adrias*, and she made a run at full speed across Scapa Flow; *Relentless* swept in, turned and fired eight torpedoes. Practice torpedoes had blowheads on them, and when they finished their run these blowheads blew the water out and the torpedo came to the surface floating vertically in the water. The blowheads were painted red and made it fairly easy to pick up torpedoes. In this instance only four torpedoes surfaced. The gunner T in charge of the torpedoes realised, to his horror, that from one of the torpedo mountings, four torpedoes had been fired with the stop valves closed. This is very bad news, because it prevents the torpedoes from running properly. The torpedo works through compressed air in the air bottles being expanded so much by ignited fuel that the air drives the motor of the torpedo. Stop valves have to be opened before the torpedo is fired, to enable the air to get out and be subjected to heat and therefore expand. If the torpedo is fired with the stop valves closed none of this happens, and the torpedo just sinks to the bottom.

So, the ship returned to the destroyer place in Scapa Flow, Gutter Sound, and went to a buoy—or at least that was the intention. In the event, trying to get to a buoy in Gutter Sound was rather unsuccessful. I have already said something about the inexperience of the crew; this was vividly demonstrated in our attempts to make fast to the buoy in Gutter Sound. This was supposed to be done by the destroyer lowering a boat; the boat then took a picking up wire from the ship to the buoy and hooked on to the buoy. The ship could then be manoeuvred up to the buoy using this picking up wire, and then the anchor cables could be secured to the buoy. By the time we got into Gutter Sound after this rather terrible torpedo firing exercise, it was dark, it was blowing a gale and it was snowing. The boat—the whaler from the starboard side of the ship—was lowered into the water, and the fellows made an awful mess of things, so that the whaler made no progress against the wind, and eventually drifted ashore on the island of Flotta. Next, the port whaler was lowered and exactly the same thing happened. It was very difficult to keep the ship in position on the buoy. However, as the Captain was a pretty good ship handler, he managed to keep the position. Then it was decided to lower the motor boat. The motor boat was lowered; its engine stopped, and the motor boat ended up ashore on the lee shore. So, now the ship had no more boats available to take a picking up rope to the buoy, and it was decided the best thing would be to leave Gutter Sound and make our way out into the Flow. I remember standing on the bridge with the Captain, as we felt our way out along Gutter Sound to make our way out into the open Scapa Flow. It was pretty awful, and we didn't really know exactly where we were. We did have radar and we could see the gap leading out into the open Flow. By this time it was snowing quite heavily and visibility was very low. To our horror, halfway along the narrow part of the gap leading out into the Flow we met a battleship coming the other way with her searchlights pointing up into the sky so that any other ships could see her, and there was nothing for it. The Captain decided, I think wisely, that the best thing to do was to turn to starboard and drop the anchor, which is what we did. To make matters worse, the chaps on the fo'c'sle reported that we had dropped the anchor through one of the submarine defence booms which were put around the battleships at that time. This was a serious problem. It was fine as long as the ship was lying the way she was, away from the boom, but the wind eventually began to veer round. We realised that soon the ship would go right over the boom and foul her propellers. The only thing we could do was slip the anchor, which we did. We then managed to get the ship out into open Scapa Flow, and anchored quite close to a little shallow patch in the middle of the Flow called the Barrel of Butter. So, there we were, lying to a single anchor in a full gale and blizzard in the middle of Scapa Flow, with no boats, only one anchor and only four of our eight torpedoes.

It had been made known to the ship that our next job was to go on a Russian convoy, and quite frankly I was not looking forward to this because the ship was still not properly worked up, and the crew were really very inexperienced. This was high winter and it would have been a much less arduous business taking a convoy to Russia in the high winter than in the summer. However, the prospect was not all that appealing. As morning broke the Captain decided that in order to get his ship back into reasonable shape, he would have to go and recover the boats and his anchor if he possibly could, and get four torpedoes to replace the ones that had been lost. In addition, by this time the ship had used up quite a lot of bunker fuel so it was decided that we should go and try to replenish the bunkers right up to the top for the next operation—this Russian convoy. Getting the boats back was not too much of a problem; one of the other destroyers very kindly lent us a boat to take men ashore to get the two whalers and the motor boat, and eventually we recovered all three. Next, we had to go alongside the oiler which, as I remember, was lying right up at the top of Gutter Sound. By this time, the wind had picked up again, and it was blowing at least a half gale, if not a full gale, which meant that the oiler lying to her anchor was rolling quite a bit. As I have said, Captain was a good ship handler, and he made a very reasonable approach alongside the oiler, got a wire out from the fo'c'sle, and everything seemed to be going well when the sailors lost the turns on the bollard of the wire and it all went shooting over the side. The destroyer veered off, and we had to make another round turn and come up again alongside the oiler. This time things did not work out at all, and the oiler rolled so much that the corner of her fo'c'sle tore into the side of *Relentless* and ripped a long hole in our fo'c'sle plating.

So there we were: a brand new destroyer, with only one anchor, half her torpedoes missing and a long gash in her forecastle plating. The Captain had the unenviable job of taking his ship alongside the destroyer depot ship in Scapa, the *Maidstone*. The depot ship flew the flag of Rear

Admiral Burnet, the admiral in charge of all the home fleet destroyers. I remember well this red-faced admiral looking down on us from his quarter deck, as *Relentless* came alongside and our poor Captain had to repair on board the flag ship and do his best to explain away his mishaps.

There was a piece of equipment that was supposed to detect metal in the sea, and I was instructed to take one of the drifters, which had been attached to the home fleet in Scapa Flow, and to go and search for the missing torpedoes. The torpedo run against the Greek destroyer, *Adrias*, had been made at full speed. We had no idea of the exact position of the ship when the torpedoes were fired, so I had to search over a fairly wide area of Scapa Flow with this strange piece of equipment towing behind the drifter, watching a dial to see a swing of the needle. There was no swing of the needle. I spent all day, in very bad weather, in this drifter looking for the four torpedoes, and as far as I know those four torpedoes are still lying on the bottom of Scapa Flow.

As far as I recall, the ship, having lost her place as part of the escort of the convoy going to Russia, was instructed to join the escort of a convoy coming back from Russia. Although in the Arctic, this was a much easier task than the previous experience I had had in *Keppel*, because the Germans concentrated all their efforts on the laden convoys carrying war equipment to Russia, and paid little attention to the empty ships coming back. We had an almost entirely peaceful time in the Arctic, and of course since it was midwinter the conditions were quite different to those I remembered from PQ17 in *Keppel*. Instead of having 24-hour daylight, we had 24-hour darkness in the high latitudes, and of course the German aircraft were quite incapable of doing their business in the way they had in the high summer.

On return to Scapa Flow, it was decided that the temporary repairs that had been done to the ship's fo'c'sle to repair the tear that we had suffered coming alongside the oiler should be properly repaired. The ship went down to Liverpool for this to be done. As I recall, the ship was able to give a short leave to the ship's company, since it was known that we were going out east to join the eastern fleet and that we would be away for a very long time. I think that the whole ship's company wanted to see their families and explain that we would probably be gone for years.

In due time the ship was properly repaired and fully back in first-class trim, and we started our voyage out taking a convoy down to go round the Cape of Good Hope. The escorts bunkered in Freetown, Sierra Leone and, as far as I remember, the convoy went on independently without escort. So *Relentless* was then running as a single ship on the rest of her passage down to Cape Town. As far as I recall we were doing about 18 knots, which is the maximum speed you can do with an ASDIC sweep. The anti-submarine device ASDIC was housed in a dome which was lowered through the bottom of the ship into the sea, and the ASDIC operator swept an oscillator round stopping every five degrees and this gave an anti-submarine sweep ahead of the ship. The dome could not be kept lowered at speeds above 18 knots for two reasons: firstly, the water noise would became so intense nothing else could be heard, and secondly, there was a severe strain on the mountings of the dome at high speed.

We must have been going, as I say, at 18 knots when there was a serious jolt in the ship. I was on watch at the time, and looking astern I could see a mangled dead whale surface. Not only, I think, had the whale been hit by the ASDIC dome, but he had also suffered some further damage from the destroyer's propellers. The result was that the ASDIC dome was torn off the bottom of the ship, and the lower compartment filled with water. A signal was sent to the flag officer, in West Africa, to the effect that we had hit a whale coming down the Bight of Benin at speed, and that repairs were required. It was quite obvious from the signal back from the admiral in charge of naval affairs in West Africa that he didn't think much of this story of hitting a whale. He therefore signalled to the ship to come into Lagos for investigation. This we did, and in the outer harbour, the pool outside the main port of Lagos, fellows came off to inspect the ship and see what had in fact happened. I am quite sure that the naval authorities thought that it was not a whale that we had hit, but that the ship had grounded somewhere and we were trying to excuse the matter.

It was my first experience of West Africa and I didn't like it. I have had a lot to do with West Africa in my later life and I have never revised my opinion. To my mind it is one of the most unattractive parts of the world. The climate is really awful—I don't like hot weather or wet weather—the West African climate seemed to be very commonly dull leaden skies, very high humidity and temperatures somewhere about 90 degrees Fahrenheit.

By this time, the remains of the whale in the bottom of the ship had suffered quite a lot of deterioration, and the smell was absolutely awful. At least it immediately convinced the authorities that the ship had hit a whale and that something had to be done. At that time Nigeria was a British colony, and the nautical affairs in Nigeria were handled by a very competent body of people, the Nigerian Marine. The naval authorities asked the Nigerian Marine to see to the removal of all the remains of the whale from the bottom of the ship and to fit a new ASDIC dome. This gave rise to a considerable amount of difficulty, because it was quite obvious that the ship would have to be docked for this job to be done. The biggest floating dock that was available to the Nigerian Marine in Lagos at that time was not sufficiently large to lift the destroyer completely out of the water. It was therefore decided that the ship would be put into the dry dock, the dry dock would be lifted up underneath the ship, but the ship would not come completely out of the water. This meant the destroyer was lying in the floating dock in the intense heat, with the awful smell for a number of days while divers used the dock as a platform to scrape out all the horrible whale remains and get the pieces of the broken ASDIC dome out so that they could fit the new dome. This took about a week, and it was perhaps the worst week that I spent in all my time in *Relentless*, because there was absolutely no ventilation, there was this awful heat and this dreadful smell and everyone in the ship was thoroughly fed up. We spent as much time as possible ashore. Certainly there were some most attractive beaches that we could go to outside Lagos harbour on the Atlantic coast, and we tried to spend as much time as we could there, but there was no avoiding the fact that one had to sleep in the ship, and that was very unpleasant indeed.

There was a very pleasant club in Lagos, and some of my fellow officers and I were enjoying the hospitality offered to us there, when I was surprised to hear a voice I thought I recognised singing a very rude Scottish song. It was my cousin Norman Porter who was commissioned as a medical officer in the King's African Rifles. We spent quite a few happy hours together there.

In due time a new ASDIC dome was fitted, the dry dock was lowered and we were very glad to say goodbye to the port of Lagos and continue our way down to Cape Town.

The Eastern Fleet that the ship was going to join had, at this time, retreated from Singapore back to Mombasa on the east coast of Africa, and the Japanese were not very active in the Indian Ocean. So the eastern fleet was simply building up strength before going back to the base at Trincomalee so that the Japanese naval forces could be engaged. It was therefore decided that our destroyer flotilla, the eleventh destroyer flotilla, should stay in South Africa running convoys around the Cape from Cape Town to Durban and back the other way. As far as we were concerned this was a very pleasant duty indeed. There had been a certain amount of U-boat activity, and a number of ships had in fact been torpedoed south of the South African Cape. However, the conditions were so different from the Atlantic that it was almost unbelievably pleasant, voyaging backwards and forwards between Cape Town and Durban.

The captain in charge of the flotilla—Captain Hilary Worthington Biggs, another formidable destroyer captain—decided to make his headquarters in Durban, and so we received all our instructions in Durban. We found the South African people so hospitable it was unbelievable. This went on for eight months, so we became friendly with a number of people in both Cape Town and Durban. A number of us had girlfriends in Cape Town, and I remember we used to go to dances in the Western Provinces sports club, which was a beautiful place. We used to dress in mess undress for these dances, with white mess coats. It was all very splendid, and quite unlike the war that I had known up until that time. The third lieutenant in *Relentless* was a South African whose home was in Durban, so he introduced us to a lot of people there, and we had a good time during the eight months whilst we were busy running convoys around the Cape.

As I have said, the South African people were incredibly hospitable, and this applied to the whole of the ship's company. When we gave leave, which we did at least once during our eight month stay there, I recall there was a lady who was on the *Cape Times* staff, who as a social duty took it upon herself to arrange holidays for the ship's company to be accommodated all over South Africa, and arranged for fares to be paid. The sailors could not believe the hospitality that was offered to them; it was so generous, and so wonderful for them to get away from the ship, where they were cooped up in mess decks, and spend some time with South African families. They went all over the country to people who were prepared to take them in.

I was fortunate in that I had a cousin living in Johannesburg and I remember I spent my leave with her. She had a family of young children and I got to know these youngsters quite well, and used to have a lot of fun with them. I remember they were desperately anxious that I should wear uniform whenever I went out with them. I'm bound to say that my preference was to wear an old pair of flannels and a shirt but on one occasion they prevailed on me to don full number ten uniform—consisting of white long trousers and white uniform coat with brass buttons and epaulettes. I had taken them out in a boat in the zoo lake in Zoo Park in Johannesburg, and we had come in ready to go back home for lunch. I was just stepping out of the boat onto a little jetty, when the children pushed the boat off, with the result that I stepped right into the lake. I had to walk back to the house covered in duck weed in my beautiful number ten white suit.

My time in South Africa was undoubtedly the happiest of the war. But all good things have to come to an end, and it was eventually decided that the eastern fleet would move to Trincomalee. The eleventh destroyer flotilla was to stop the pleasant business of taking convoys around the Cape, and join the fleet in Trincomalee.

Trincomalee is a really magnificent natural harbour, with deep water, an easily protected entrance and a wonderful anchorage for the fleet. There was a line of buoys, on which the destroyers lay, a buoy ahead and a buoy astern. The various destroyer flotillas all had their own string of buoys. This meant our social life largely consisted of various ships in the flotilla entertaining their friends from the other ships. Any time we were in harbour we had pretty wild parties. We had had a lot of girlfriends while we were in South Africa, but the female availability in Trincomalee was extremely limited. There were a few nurses and a few WRNS, but not very many, and the girls were very much sought after, so in *Relentless* we decided that we would have no ladies on board the ship at all. This had the strange effect that the girls who knew about the ban that we had put on their delightful presence tried to get invitations to the ship. We resisted this and only relented on special occasions like ship's company concerts. *Relentless* was in fact very good at ship's company concerts.

Recreational activity in Trincomalee was extremely limited, and the only thing that was appealing at all was that there was a beach outside the harbour, which was quite pleasant. We used to spend some afternoons there swimming and enjoying the beach. Very often, we returned to the ship by swimming about three-quarters of a mile. When the ship first went to Trincomalee there was a lot of worry about shark, because there were a large number of sharks in the harbour. We used to see their dorsal fins cutting the water; nevertheless when the fleet was in harbour there were large numbers of sailors desperate to get into the water. In addition to just swimming over the side of the ship, most ships had long poles which could be put over the ship's side to support water polo goals. Inter-ship matches were very popular. There was a lot of thought given to the dangers involved with sharks, and at first marksmen were put in strategic positions in the various ships with rifles, in order to try to discourage sharks. In fact, as the time went on, months became years; there was never an occasion where any person was attacked by a shark, and there were thousands of sailors swimming in the water all the time.

As I said before, the officers had a certain amount of social life, partying between the various ships in their own flotilla or even other ships at anchor in the harbour. The sailors had very little in the way of social activity or amusement of any kind. There was a canteen ashore, which was a terrible place—it was a corrugated iron building and very hot. The only decoration was ship's crests, and the sailors were given ration tickets which enabled them to have a few pints of beer; but it was pretty awful. So a lot of our efforts were concentrated on trying to provide water activities, and we used to have very large-scale fleet regattas, both sailing and pulling oars. These were of great interest to all the ships of the fleet, and it was quite common to have 30 or 40 whalers or cutters engaged in regattas. The interest in the outcome of the various races in the regattas we held in Trincomalee was enhanced by the fact that large amounts of money used to be staked on the various boats from the different ships. Destroyers only carried whalers; it was only the larger ships which carried cutters, but it was thought to be very *infra dig* to bet on any other ship's boat in a regatta where boats of your own ship were involved.

At that time, the eastern fleet was under the command of a very distinguished officer, Admiral Sir Bruce Fraser, and I believe it was he who had the idea of allocating to each ship a plot of land in which the sailors could garden and grow whichever crops they pleased. I remember that the various plots of land allocated to the ships in the eleventh destroyer flotilla, the R-class destroyers, were all side by side. Some of the other ships in the flotilla thought they should try to grow crops with which they were familiar, for instance, lettuces and cabbages. However, in *Relentless* we felt that the smart thing was to grow crops that would suit the particular climate in that part of the world, and we planted a lot of pawpaws. The advantage of the pawpaw tree is that if you stand and watch it you can practically see it growing. The result of this was that the *Relentless* ship's company were able to harvest quite a significant crop of ripe pawpaws. It is a very nice fruit in the tropics, and very much esteemed by *Relentless*'s ship's company.

I have already mentioned ship's company concerts and here again *Relentless* seemed to have a good way of staging these; we became, in the eastern fleet, quite famous for ship's company concerts. I remember one of the best ones we had was in the port of Aden. We must have been escorting some carriers, I can't remember exactly what, but we did finish up in the port of Aden and there we gave a ship's company concert. The ship had been given an upright piano. I think we got the piano before we left the United Kingdom, donated perhaps by the town to which the ship was attached. The piano was normally kept in the mess deck and the ship's company concert was always held on the fore part of the ship; it was a major problem to get the piano from the mess deck up onto the fore part. In fact it had to be right up in the eyes of the ship where the stage was and all the audience then sat under A gun, which was the forward gun, on bench trestles. So, getting the piano involved wheeling it out from the mess deck, getting both of the ship's whalers with wooden beams across between the two whalers, rigging the piano on a pair of sheer legs, and lowering it over the ship's side down onto the whalers. It was a very tricky operation. Then we had to move the two whalers, with the piano on the beams between them up to where it was required on the fo'c'sle head, religging the sheer legs, then hoisting the piano up and swinging it over into its position for the ship's company concert.

The sailors really loved these concerts, and no-one loved them more than the chief stoker, who was a very large man—he must have been all of sixteen stone. He decided that the stokers in the ship would put on a fairy display and this chief stoker was going to be the queen of the fairies. His idea was that the fairies would appear on the stage and the queen, the chief stoker, would fly down onto the stage. He aimed to do this by coming down the forestay of the ship with a shackle over the forestay, and him sitting in a bosun's chair. He was lowered down by a rope attached to the base of the foremast. The event went very well, with his stokers, the fairies, all bustling about the stage. He, the fairy queen, was dressed in an immaculate garb, he had a wig made out of teased out rope yarns, and his brassiere was filled with the points of brass high angled shell caps. He had a little skirt and he was very heavily made up. The idea, as I say, was that he was going to fly down onto the stage, lowered down the forestay in his bosun's chair. The chap who had the job of lowering him down the forestay lost the turns of his rope; the poor old chief stoker came down the last 20 feet onto the stage in a whirr, and landed in considerable discomfort with a tremendous thump on the stage. The engineer in the ship had cast him a fairy wand by making a star out of cast iron fixed onto a broom handle, and the chief stoker, in his dazed condition, picked up his fairy wand and swung round to address the assembled audience, hitting one of the other fairies on the side of the head with his wand and knocking him absolutely stone cold. This was, of course, enormously appreciated by the audience who didn't really know that the whole thing was quite unrehearsed and wasn't at all planned. In fact, the chap who had been hit on the head with the cast iron star was in pretty poor shape, and he was taken off to the sick bay. He was not seriously damaged, but he was unable to take any further part in the fun enjoyed by the rest of the ship's company.

The Captain had invited some dignitaries from the Port of Aden to attend this concert; these people were most impressed and pressed us very hard to come ashore in Aden to one of their halls in the small town of Aden and put on the show there. I was to some extent in charge of the concert party, and I felt that whilst it was a great success in the ship where the sailors were extremely appreciative, whether or not things went right, having the concert in a place other than the fore end of the ship would be wrong. I decided it was sensible to refuse the invitation to take the concert party ashore, with which the others agreed.

Relentless was given the interesting commission of taking some district officers from Malaya to the Cocos and Keeling Islands, which lie south of Sumatra, to see whether the local population would be agreeable to fortification of these islands by a force of Royal Marines. The purpose of this was to obviate the difficulty that would arise if the Japanese managed to use these islands as a naval base, which apparently the powers that be thought they might be prepared to do.

As I recall, *Relentless* arrived about ten o'clock in the morning and dropped anchor in the wonderful natural harbour. A boat was sent into the main village on what was known as the home island to bring off some people, to discuss with these Malay-speaking district officers that we had on board, the possibility of British military presence on the island. The Malay chaps who came off from the main village were very distinguished gentlemen, and they were dressed in the normal Malay garb of a sarong. It seemed slightly incongruous for us to have these gentlemen brought on board, and taken up to the Captain's cabin, and entertained with coffee, toast and marmalade.

They seemed to be quite agreeable to the proposals and everything went very smoothly. We found the Cocos and Keeling islands a most interesting part of the world. They were originally settled by a Scottish marine adventurer called Cluny Ross, who was sailing in that part of the world when he discovered these islands and thought that it would be a very good place to start a community. He then went to the coast of various other Malaysian islands and took off some willing or unwilling people, male and female, to inhabit his new territory. The source of revenue was the export of copra. Apparently, a small steamer called there at fairly irregular intervals to load this copra and that was the only cash input into the islands.

What was very interesting was that they had developed a sort of strange socialist way of conducting their affairs. Everyone on the island seemed to have a share in what was more or less an idyllic lifestyle. Young men and young women were taken from their parents when they reached the age of puberty, and were segregated onto different islands. Thereafter their efforts were to contribute to the wealth-producing part of the islands' business, that is, the export of copra. A book was kept, in which each person amassed 'points'. When they reached a certain number of points, the men were entitled to a house and a wife and they became a part of the islands' then ongoing child-raising part of the community. As I suppose with any community there were some chaps who behaved in some way which was considered, by the general councils, to be anti-social, and they were put on what was effectively a prison island.

The original Cluny Ross married a Malaysian princess and they became the ruling family over several generations. I think the present ruler of the islands was in fact away in the United Kingdom at the outbreak of war, and he married a girl from London. Generally the lifestyle of the people on the island was fairly idyllic. They had no problem in feeding themselves and making houses was a very easy matter. All they did was to use a few poles to support a house made of coconut palms.

One of the interesting things was that Cluny Ross had introduced the game of golf, not golf as known in Scotland, but it was the best he could do with what was available. I think the golf clubs were made out of the fronds of coconuts suitably hacked to look like something more like a hockey stick than a golf club; they had quite an impressive little golf course. Quite what they used for balls I don't recall.

Relentless stayed in this anchorage for several days, during which time we became quite friendly with some of the local chaps. I remember on one occasion we took them out fishing. In a destroyer in tropical waters fishing meant dropping nine ounce charges of TNT into the water, then simply picking up the fish that came to the surface after the ensuing explosion. The fellows we took with us out on these fishing trips were frightfully impressed, and they wanted to be given TNT—but it was generally felt that this would not be a very wise thing to do.

In due time, after it had been concluded that the local people were perfectly prepared to have the Royal Marines, *Relentless* left the islands. I remember thinking that in many ways the introduction of a force of Royal Marines to a more or less idyllic community would create all sorts of problems; I never really found out how well things went in the long run.

CHAPTER EIGHT

The War Against Japan

The British Eastern Fleet in Trincomalee had been building strength for some considerable time, so in due course it was thought to be appropriate to commence aggressive operations against the Japanese in their occupation, particularly of Malaysia and Java. Fleet operations have always fascinated me. For a destroyer man, it is particularly thrilling to be on the screen ahead of a vast fleet of battleships, aircraft carriers, cruisers and so on, because the fleet proceeds at high speed, and to maintain station in a destroyer when there is an alteration of course requires a high degree of relative velocity thinking and general ship control expertise.

It used to take about a full day for the entire fleet to leave Trincomolee. I remember one operation we took on was to attack the port of Sabang. Sabang is a relatively minor port in the north end of the Island of Sumatra. It was fairly heavily utilised, apparently, by the Japanese. The idea was that the fleet was to stand offshore and bombard the port, and certain destroyers from the fleet were to run in and fire torpedoes into the harbour. The operation was really very successful. We had a considerable amount of attack by Japanese aircraft but this was before the time of Kamikaze, and the Japanese did not seem to me to be up to the calibre of the Germans. Certainly, their torpedo bombers seemed not nearly as efficient as the German equivalent carrying the same sort of armament.

I recall that Admiral Bruce Fraser let it be known that he was intent on what he called trailing coats around the Japanese theatre, and on many occasions the entire fleet would put to sea from Trincomolee. We had this incredible task getting all those heavy ships and attendant destroyers out of the harbour. I remember on one occasion the eleventh destroyer flotilla, the R-class ships of which *Relentless* was one, were dispatched down the coast at a fair high speed, something like 20 knots, and I think that the command had forgotten about this until we had steamed quite a long way. This was to get the destroyers well out of the road of all the other ships leaving the harbour, and by the time it was realised that we were still steaming south at a fairly high speed, we had a hell of a job catching up with the fleet when eventually we were told to take station ahead of the main fleet. These coat trailing operations in my experience never brought any Japanese ships of any consequence to action. They did result in a fairly high amount of air attack; most of it was either dive or high level bomber, but we didn't seem to suffer any very substantial damage.

There were very brave army chaps called forward bombardment officers, and the destroyers used to take these fellows at night into about a mile off the coast of various parts of the Japanese occupied Dutch East Indies and Malaysia. We carried canvas canoes and these brave army officers would embark in these canoes, go onshore with their portable radio transmitters and determine targets to be attacked the following day. They would give us map references of these various targets and we carried out the bombardment with 4.7 shells on the targets by navigation. I was navigator of the ship and I had always had a great interest in exact navigation, so, to me, this was a fascinating business. The idea was that having pinpointed the position of the target—usually a camp of Japanese soldiers that the forward bombardment officers had located—we would mark this on a chart, and then determine a course along which the ship would have to steer very exactly. The guns would then be fired, using tables to get the range of the fall of the shell and the giro-compass in the ship to determine the angle at which the guns had to be fired. These very brave forward bombardment officers would sit somewhere where they could see the fall of shot, and they would direct the fall either left or right or up or down, as the case might be. I understand that this method of bombardment was really quite accurate, and a large amount of damage was done to various Japanese army positions. I am afraid that the brave chaps who had to go ashore to determine the target and spot the fall of shot had a rough time. We always used to try to pick them up, but in most cases we didn't. Hopefully, they were taken prisoner—but I think in many cases they were just shot.

The ships themselves involved in these bombardments did not always go unpunished. I remember one of the ships in the flotilla, not on an operation I was concerned with, but some similar operations conducted by other ships, had got fairly close inshore right in front of the Japanese 88-mm gun, and the first shell when this gun opened fire hit the destroyer engine room, with absolutely disastrous results. The engine room of these ships obviously had huge boiler capability, with very high pressure and high temperature steam. A shell bursting in the engine room was always certain to disrupt one of the steam pipes, which would cook all the poor people in the engine room, and that is exactly what happened to this

71

ship of our flotilla. However, one of the other ships in the flotilla managed to silence the Japanese gun and come in and tow the ship clear.

A fleet flotilla is divided first of all into two divisions; the first division is commanded by Captain D, and the second division is commanded by a commander who is second in command of the flotilla. The four ships are divided into two subdivisions, each with a senior ship. Our subdivisional leader was *Racehorse*, and *Racehorse* suffered a fate similar to, but not as disastrous as, the ship in the previous described incident. They were doing this inshore bombardment and a shell from a Japanese ship hit *Racehorse* in the way of the sponsons carrying the anti-aircraft guns. The first lieutenant was on deck—the first lieutenant in ships of this type usually had responsibility for damage control—and he was very anxious that he should be on site if the ship was hit in any particular compartment, to do whatever he could to minimise the damage. He was in the way of this shell which hit the sponsons of the anti-aircraft guns; the scupper pipe taking water down from the anti-aircraft gun-deck was blown apart by the shell, and a bit of the pipe hit him in the bottom. I remember that he was in hospital in Simonstown when we went back there, I imagine for boiler clean. We went to visit him in hospital, and I remember that he found it very embarrassing to be visited by various ladies from Cape Town who enquired as to the nature of his wounds. He said that he felt that he couldn't really say that he'd been hit in the arse with a drain pipe, which is what had happened.

Another operation I remember very well was when we were for some reason—I can't remember exactly why—lying in grand harbour Mauritius, and a signal from the Admiralty came to the effect that there was a German supply ship operating in the Indian Ocean. She was a tanker, a ship called the *Charlotte Schliemann*, which had been refitted in Japan. She was reported to be heavily armed with five 5.1-inch guns, and was operating with a substantial number of U-boats in the Indian Ocean and carrying spare crews, spare torpedoes and fuel. I imagine that there had been some espionage work in Japan, or in some part of the world, where people had gained information to which they obviously shouldn't have had access, and we were given a position where this ship was thought to be operating, and Catalina aircraft to search the area. Catalina aircraft were very efficient long-range flying boats. They provided an excellent aerial platform of visibility over the sea. In due time the Catalina reported that she had made contact with a ship that was thought to be this *Charlotte Schliemann*. The aircraft reported that the ship was flying the Swedish flag. The aircraft then signalled *Relentless*, to the effect that he didn't have enough fuel to stay with the *Charlotte Schliemann* until

Relentless could make contact. I forget the distances, but it was some considerable distance away from *Relentless's* then position. Our Captain sent a signal to the Catalina to the effect that he had to stay with the German supply ship until *Relentless* got there, even if it meant that he had to land his aircraft in the sea, since *Relentless* would easily be able to pick up the crew, so there would be no problem. The Captain of the aircraft said that he wasn't prepared to do this; he thought that the conditions were such that landing in the sea would hazard his aircraft and crew. He said was going to stay as long as he possibly could, reporting the position of the ship, but he would eventually have to leave when he was at his minimum fuel for return to his base in Mauritius, and he would then signal his best-known position of the ship and depart. There was a further exchange of signals, where the Captain of *Relentless* pleaded with him to stay on site, but that was not successful, so the aircraft left in due course, giving us his best-known position of the *Charlotte Schliemann*.

It was my job as navigator to then lay on what is called a Vignolls curve of search, which is a matter of estimating roughly the direction which the ship will take at an assumed speed, and then radiating spokes in the assumed direction, plotting on each hour the ship's possible position depending on the course that she had taken. It was a beautiful moonlight night, with excellent visibility, and the Captain of *Relentless* had decided, in the event I think very wisely, that when the ship was sighted we would run in at maximum speed, turn and fire torpedoes. We would not make any effort to establish identity. We had carefully checked with the Admiralty that there were no ships in the area other than this German supply ship, and we sincerely hoped that this was true. In terms of guns, the *Charlotte Schliemann* was thought to have five 5.1 guns, while *Relentless* had four 4.7s, so we were substantially outgunned. It would have been very unwise indeed to go and try to determine the identity of the ship, since if she opened fire we would be likely to get a pounding. In due time, at a range of 11 miles, we sighted the *Charlotte Schliemann*; as had been planned we ran in, turned a mile and a half off and I fired eight torpedoes. It was a marvellous opportunity; I had never had to do a torpedo attack before, and it was a great thrill to have a ship turn and fire eight torpedoes. The *Charlotte Schliemann*, we later discovered, had assumed that *Relentless* was a cruiser, and they didn't want to open fire because they thought they would be outgunned. Before they knew it, they were hit by two of the torpedoes, and before they could take any substantial action the ship was listing and sinking. I believe that they had decided that rather than let the ship be captured, they would detonate demolition charges. We never found out whether they actually did this. In any case, within a few minutes the ship was going down into the Indian Ocean. None of the crew got into boats; they were all swimming about in the sea. *Relentless* stopped and we picked up some 50 of the crew, some of them were spare U-boat crews, while some were German naval people who were the crew of the supply ship. Then one of the lookouts in *Relentless* said that he thought he saw a periscope, and that was the end of that. I don't know if the report was true or not, but it would obviously have been very unwise for *Relentless* to stay around picking up survivors if there was a U-boat in the vicinity. It is quite possible there was a U-Boat, because the ship was known to have been supplying U-boats immediately before she was sighted by the Catalina.

We had picked up some 50 of the Germans from this ship; all we could do was clear the lower mess deck where the stokers normally lived, and put all the Germans down below. The officers were kept separately in various cabins. As Navigator, I normally slept in the charthouse at sea, so the old Captain of the German ship—he was probably about 35, but he seemed to me to be old at that time—stayed in my usual cabin which I didn't use when we were at sea. It was very interesting that a number of the ship's crew had had their houses bombed, and were very anti-German. At first the crew were very hostile to these Germans; however, since there was only one hatch up from the stoker's mess deck into the upper mess deck, it was really very easy to maintain control. The Germans were instructed that they had to do everything that our sailors had to do. They had to keep their messes properly cleaned and ordered, and do their cooking just as our sailors did. They were given supplies, and had to decide what they wanted to eat, and then they had to prepare their food and have it sent up to the galley. We were in the habit of making rounds; every officer coming off watch had a look down into the mess decks to see that everything was all right, and in no time at all we found our sailors were becoming very friendly with these Germans. I suppose it is understandable that they felt that once they had made some sort of a personal contact, they found that they were very much of a kind, and very quickly the problem was to limit the amount of fraternisation that was going on. The sailors were going to this German mess deck and playing cards, and taking them down bars of chocolate and cups of cocoa. I remember on one occasion going my rounds, and to my horror I saw a British sailor hand a sub-machine gun to a German as he came up the ladder, so the German could pass the gun up to him. We had to be very careful about the degree of fraternisation. I have already said that the Captain of the German ship was accommodated in my cabin. I used to go down there every morning to do my washing, have a bath and shave, and I got talking to this chap and found him a very interesting fellow. He said that he was appreciative of the fact that we had been quite punctilious about the treatment of these prisoners. Since their ship had been fitted out in Japan, they had acquired all sorts of valuable things. Most of them had beautiful solid gold demesne cigarette cases, and we collected all these items and put them in the ship's safe, and said that in due time we would give them back their valuables. The Captain of the German ship thought this was very decent. He and I used to spend quite a bit of time chatting about this and that, and it was obvious to me that his feelings and thoughts about the war were very similar to my own. We were both sailors, we had a job to do and we did it to the best of our ability. We had no desperate hate for the opposing forces.

Our next problem was to get rid of the German prisoners, because quite obviously, having had to clear out the lower mess deck made the upper mess deck severely overcrowded. The chaps were having difficulty finding a slinging berth for hammocks, so we were most anxious to get rid of these men at the first opportunity. We went back to Mauritius, and as the sailors had by this time told the Germans about playing water polo when the ship was in harbour, the Germans thought this was a very good idea and had challenged the *Relentless* ship's company to a game. This was thought to be a reasonable request, since they had been in the lower mess deck for quite a long time, the weather was very hot and the ship was like a tin box in the bright sunshine and the mess decks were extremely unpleasant. It was thought to be quite fair to allow these German chaps up on the deck; they picked a team and *Relentless* picked a team, the water polo poles were put out on the long rods over the ship's side and the water polo match was soon in full swing. Our Captain had gone ashore to report his proceedings to the naval captain in charge of the base in Mauritius, who was a retired captain who had been called back to colours at the outbreak of war. He was a very stiff and very punctilious sort of naval officer. According to him, he had come by to survey the prisoners, and was absolutely horrified and very furious to find that the German prisoners were in the water playing water polo with *Relentless*'s ship's crew. He made his feelings very well known.

We obviously had to suspend operations, and the poor old Germans were all tucked away down to the mess deck while a formal inspection was carried out with the British blue jackets parading around with their guns. We were, however, quite unable to find any way of getting rid of them in Mauritius; there was apparently no way that so many prisoners could be taken off our hands. The next occasion was when the ship went into Mombasa, and there it was agreed that the German prisoners would be turned over to the army. Before this happened we decided that we would do what we had said we would do, and give them back all their valuables. The German prisoners, by this time, had come to the conclusion that it would be sensible for them to make these valuables available to the ship's company with whom they had become very friendly, because they said that if they didn't the army would just pinch them and that would be that. However, we decided that that wasn't our problem and they had to reassume responsibility for their valuables man by man which is what they did, and they were taken off to go to some prison camp in Kenya.

In due time, of course, we had to report to Captain D and his staff about the whole operation, and I remember the torpedo officer, who was a very nice man and more or less a friend of mine, saying, 'We think what you did was OK but why the hell did you fire eight torpedoes, surely you could have managed with two; do you know that these torpedoes cost £2,000 each?' That sticks very much in my memory, because certainly for a more or less impecunious lieutenant in the Royal Navy in those days £2,000 was a lot of money, but on the other hand firing two torpedoes would reduce the risk of hitting the ship very substantially. It seemed to me that it was perfectly reasonable to fire all eight torpedoes because the spread would ensure the possibility of a hit on the ship, and as I have said, we were aware of the fact that if we had to engage in a gun fight after the torpedoes had been fired at this ship we would have been in pretty bad shape.

About this time the first lieutenant of *Relentless* was relieved, a man called Brian Longbottom, and I was promoted to First Lieutenant of *Relentless*. The first lieutenant's job in a ship is to look after the cleaning, repairs and maintenance of the ship and to supervise, arrange and control all the drills of the fighting equipment of the ship. It is a very interesting job and it was strange in a way that I had never had any formal training in gunnery or torpedo or anti-aircraft gunnery at all. It was a matter of on the job learning but I suppose that on the job learning in wartime is not a bad way of getting the necessary knowledge. I can remember being quite worried about my gunnery responsibilities, because *Relentless* had quite a sophisticated gunnery control arrangement and I had to devote quite a lot of time and effort to understanding in adequate depth all the various bits and pieces of the gunnery equipment in the ship.

In the Navy the relationship between the commissioned officers and the other ranks was, I believe, very good. I mentioned earlier these forward bombardment officers from the army, with whom we had a lot of chat when we were taking them over for operations against the

Japanese and one of the things that they remarked on was the much higher degree of communication, friendship and understanding there was in the Navy between commissioned and non-commissioned ranks. This was rather different to their experience in the army where the relationship between commissioned and non-commissioned personnel was rather formal, and there was very little friendship across that divide. Certainly, I found in taking over my new responsibility, I got a lot of help from the petty officers who were experienced and knowledgeable of all that had to be done and how it had to be done.

About this time a Commodore Destroyers was appointed to the Eastern Fleet, with responsibility for the efficiency of the whole destroyer command. When the fleet went to sea Commodore Destroyers decided that he would like to lead his destroyer force from a suitable ship and he chose *Relentless*. Why he chose *Relentless* I don't really know, but quite obviously he couldn't take one of the flotilla leaders of the several flotillas that were attached at that time to the Eastern Fleet; he had to take a private ship, and in his wisdom he selected *Relentless*. This was interesting, in that we were then carrying the Flag Officer, the Commodore in charge of the whole destroyer force. It was bad news in that he brought a substantial staff with him, which meant that they had to be accommodated, and a lot of the junior officers in *Relentless* then had to sling hammocks, which they didn't like very much, and the wardroom was very overcrowded. The Commodore used the Captain's harbour cabin when the ship was at sea, but his officers obviously used the wardroom and the ship was very heavily overcrowded. However it was quite good news for me, because as far as I remember a lieutenant's pay in those days was 28 shillings a day, and I got an extra one and sixpence for being the executive officer of the ship, plus another one and sixpence for being the executive officer of a flagship. So, carrying the Commodore was very beneficial for me in financial terms. Of course, if there was no fleet operation on hand he went ashore, and we reverted to being a private ship.

Lieutenant Commander Fell had been our captain from the time the ship was built until he was relieved by Lieutenant Commander Barstow. They were both very fine destroyer officers, and people that I admired and got along with very well. One of the problems was to try to keep the sailors reasonably happy and contented, and one of the things we did, I remember, was to have a brains trust. We used to select people for it; the doctor was always a very popular man to have on the brains trust because there were all sorts of questions with a medical background, and some of them very strange. A few of us used to sit around the table, and one of the senior petty officers would collect questions, sifting out the ones that he thought were completely inappropriate. Any question that related to the running or the discipline of the ship was thought to be inappropriate. The Chief Petty Officer would read out the question and the brains trust would make the best they could of it. All this was transmitted over loudspeakers to the various mess decks. It was quite a good way of maintaining morale and trying to ensure that the ship's company functioned as a unit and everybody felt responsible and friendly to everybody else.

One of the most important jobs that a first lieutenant had to do was to keep the ship looking spick and span and this I very much enjoyed doing. It was a matter of considerable pride to try and keep one's ship the best that one possibly could in comparison with the other ships in the destroyer division, and in particular with the ships in your own flotilla. We used to do our repairs either in India or South Africa. South Africa was by far the most popular, and if the ship could get some mission which took her anywhere near it was really very nice to have a boiler clean in South Africa, where we could resume contact with some of the friends that we had made during our time of conducting convoys around the Cape.

Bombay was the other alternative; there was a very competent naval dockyard in Bombay, and the first lieutenants of the various ships always tried to get bits and pieces which would make their ship look more attractive than the other ships in the flotilla. I remember one of the tricks that we used to get up to, which was rather bad in a way, was to get a wooden spurnwater fitted around the edge of the upper deck of the ship. The problem if you didn't have a spurnwater was that the dirty water coming over the ship's side stained it and made the ship look much less elegant. I remember Bombay was a very good place to be able to impress the dockyard how necessary it was to have this fitted. Really, it was a bad thing to do—any wood in ships was bad news, because if a shell exploded anywhere near wood there would be splinters flying in all directions—but we didn't think too much about that. It was very interesting that the American ships had no wood on them at all. I believe that is the case in the British Navy now, but at that time big ships, battleships and cruisers, all had wooden decks, so we didn't worry too much about the inclusion of a little bit of wood in destroyers.

I remember one of the other ships in the flotilla succeeded in persuading the dockyard in Bombay to give them a rather beautiful ensign staff with a gorgeous crown on the top of it. I have said that when the flotilla was in harbour in Trincomalee the officers used to visit various ships; very often this was done by simply climbing down onto the buoy and up the stern line of the ship next door and arriving uninvited in their wardroom. We used to have fairly drunken parties, I'm afraid, and it was common to pinch things from other ships to enhance the value or appearance of one's own. I remember that we managed after some difficulty to pinch this beautiful ensign staff that our flotilla mate had had made in the dockyard in Bombay, and make out of it a boom for the Captain's skimming dinghy. It looked very nice, I must say, but it was much to the annoyance of the ship that had lost its much prized ensign staff.

Around the early part of 1945 the ship went back to Simonstown for another periodical repair of some kind, and I was relieved to come home. I stayed in Cape Town until a suitable ship could be made available for me to return to the United Kingdom. In the event it was the *Mauritania*, which had been used for trooping across the Atlantic. She had a contingent of American soldiers on board who were responsible for troops embarked in the ship. They weren't used to carrying naval personnel, and soon after we boarded the ship it became clear that relationships between the Americans in charge of the troops and the naval chaps being repatriated to the UK were not too good. I remember that the first lieutenant of *Racehorse* was travelling with me; he and I were pretty good chums by this time. He was a fellow who didn't suffer fools gladly, and as he said to me, we had been first lieutenants of fleet destroyers. We reckoned that we were fellows of some reasonable substance and should not be ordered about by these American GIs, who were very punctilious about everything they thought had to be done in the ship. My friend had gone out on the deck and was smoking a cigarette, and one of these American GIs came along and threatened him with a truncheon. A lot of thought in destroyers had been given to the question of naked lights, and the effect they could have on ships being detected during hours of darkness. It was found that lighting a match was not on; you should never light a match in the open because the flame of a match, or a lighter, could be seen at a greater distance than you could see the hull of the ship. However, in any condition of darkness a glowing cigarette was not of greater visibility than the hull of the ship, so it was commonplace for destroyer people to smoke their cigarettes on watch or on deck. So my friend was not about to be taken to task by this American soldier, and having been threatened with the truncheon Lieutenant MacIntyre (who had been first lieutenant in *Racehorse*, and incidentally the chap who had suffered severe damage to his rear end during operations off the eastern coast of Malaysia), took the GI's truncheon and threw it over the side. The American soldier was used to exercising absolute discipline over troops carried by the ship and he reported this to his superior officer who I think was a lieutenant colonel of the US army, i.e., the officer in charge of troops. The colonel thought this was a pretty dreadful offence that MacIntyre had committed, and he referred the whole matter to the captain of the *Mauritania* who had ultimate authority. This was blown out of all proportion to what had happened. However, the captain of the *Mauritania* was a man obviously used to dealing with recalcitrant and difficult passengers, and he succeeded in sorting the matter out and tried to make it clear to the American officers in charge of the troops on board that naval personnel could not be trifled with.

We really had quite a good time in *Mauritania*. There were a number of WREN Officers on board and they provided very pleasant company for us. The food was certainly not up to what one would expect in a passenger liner of the Cunard standing; but on the other hand it was better than we had had in our destroyers, and we had a very pleasant trip home. On arrival in the United Kingdom the ship docked in Liverpool and we all went off on leave. We had been away for two and a half years, and it was very exciting and pleasant to be back in the bosom of one's family again.

The next appointment that I had was to the gunnery school and the torpedo school in the south of England, to learn about all the equipment that I had been using for months in my ship. It always seemed in the Navy that you got taught things you already knew, and never got taught things that you were about to have to undertake. However, that seemed to be the way that life was.

CHAPTER NINE

Back to Peacetime

When we arrived home from our Eastern Fleet service the war with Germany was already over, but the war in the Far East was still going on. During the courses I had to undertake for further training in modern destroyers, much emphasis was laid on the problems faced by ships with the Japanese in the Far East, particularly Kamikaze attacks, and I must say that I was not really looking forward to further service in the Eastern Fleet.

In the event, my next appointment was after peace in the Far East and my fears about being sent out to a modern destroyer in that area were not realised. I was appointed First Lieutenant of a ship called *Anthony*. The distinction about *Anthony* was that she was one of the fastest destroyers in the Navy; on a good day she could do 35 knots.

There were all sorts of differences serving in a warship in peacetime as opposed to war, and *Anthony*'s duties related to providing target practice for the Royal Air Force torpedo bombers. To do this we went all around the coast of Scotland. It really was quite enjoyable, because wherever we went the Royal Air Force seemed to think that we were having a very difficult time if we stayed at sea for more than three or four days. We would be released from further duty and allowed to go wherever we liked until the next exercise the RAF wanted to conduct. This meant that we could go into any convenient anchorage around the coast of Scotland, and very often we were invited to shoot and fish, which we enjoyed doing, by the local lairds of whatever part of the country it might be. I remember we quite often used the anchorage in Lamlash and the Duke of Montrose, the title holder of the Island of Arran at that time, invited us to shoot over his ground. In the wardroom many of us had shotguns, and we enjoyed rough shooting around Lamlash and in many other parts of Scotland. We also often went to Bangor in Northern Ireland where similar hospitality was extended to us.

About this time the Navy was contracting very substantially; *Anthony* went into Rosyth with a view to eventually paying off, and we gave a party—which is where I met my wife. This was perhaps the most fortunate thing that ever happened to me in the whole of my life, because she is a wonderful woman and I was immediately attracted to her when we first met. She, fortunately, seemed to find me not unattractive, and as I say I regard meeting her as certainly the most fortunate thing that ever happened to me.

I was eventually given command of *Anthony* but, as I say, this was very near the end of the war and nothing of much note happened.

A number of my reserve officer colleagues in the Navy decided to stay on in the service. I gave this some thought, obviously, and my girlfriend, later to become my wife, felt that I was perhaps somewhat unwise in not wanting to stay on in the Navy. However, my feelings were that the Navy was contracting; I'd had a good war and I'd been a first lieutenant of destroyers for quite a long time and eventually commanded one of them. I could see a tremendous contraction in the Navy, and I knew that the probability was that if I did join the Navy permanently I would spend a lot of my time in barracks—which I really didn't relish at all. In fact, my experience of the Navy in peacetime before the war had led me to the conclusion that it wasn't really my cup of tea.

It was not long after my demobilisation that Norma and I became engaged. My next problem was to sit some Merchant Navy examinations, because during the length of the war I had been at sea and I had no qualifications at all. This meant that I had to go to the Nautical College in Leith and start studying—which I didn't take to at all well. However, it was possible at that time for me to take all the examinations up to a Master's certificate at one go. My then fiancée and I had decided that as soon as I had got my Master's Certificate we would get married. In the event, despite my lack of studious abilities I did pass Second Mate, Mate and Master all at once. It seemed to me that the right thing for me to do then was to go on and study for Extra Master, which I had always wanted to do. An Extra Master certificate doesn't entitle one to anything more than a Master's certificate in the way of commanding merchant ships, but it does give one a lot of added theoretical information about one's chosen career and it seemed to me to be a very worthwhile thing to do. However, I may have passed my first examinations at the first attempt with relatively few problems, but when I came up against studying for Extra Master the whole thing was quite different.

Norma and I were married in a lovely old Scottish church at the west end of George Street in Edinburgh. The only thing I remember was that I was married in uniform and my sword was not in the best condition. Kneeling at the appropriate part of the ceremony I got the end of the sword scabbard stuck in the grating of the central heating system. In pulling the sword out, the brass ferrule at the end of the scabbard stuck in the grating and came off. I had some serious difficulty extracting it.

The reception after our wedding was in the Royal British Hotel in Edinburgh and it was a very splendid occasion, but here again my sword let me down. It was common for one to keep one's sword fairly well greased; I used the sword to cut the wedding cake, and the result was that there was a horrible black mark over the icing on the top of the cake.

By this time, I had run out of money; the gratuity from service in the Navy didn't last very long. Quite obviously, if I was going to continue studying for this difficult examination I would have to have some source of income. I got a job teaching radar in the Nautical College; I knew very little about the subject, but fortunately all my students knew even less. I remember that the wage scale for lecturers at that time was £435 on starting, rising by increments of £15 a year to a maximum of £650.

Norma very cleverly got us a flat at the very top of a building in Atholl Crescent, a very good address in Edinburgh, but it wasn't really up to much. We only had one room and the use of a bathroom. We were idyllically happy in many ways, although I found my studying very difficult. The lecturing wasn't very onerous in terms of time—as far as I recall one started about nine in the morning and finished about four in the afternoon—but I found teaching much more arduous than I had imagined it would be. Then when I came home at night I had to study, while my poor wife had to sit with headphones on listening to the radio so that I wouldn't be distracted from my study. Any distraction, I may say, was very welcome, but she very kindly decided that she would listen to the radio with headphones. She really found this very difficult, because if it was an amusing programme she couldn't even laugh!

The only difficulty we had was this business of studying; otherwise we were idyllically happy. We were newly married; our main source of pleasure was taking a bus to Cramond and walking along the sea front in the winter, and looking at the seals lying on the beaches along the coast of the Firth of Forth. We used to go regularly to the theatre where the cheapest seats were one and six, and that was about all we could afford with the addition of a bag of sweets.

My first attempt at passing the Extra Masters examination was a dismal failure, as was my second and I must say I got quite dispirited; however, eventually I did pass my examination.

Housing at this time was very difficult indeed. We tried to get a house similar to what our parents had had in Edinburgh and that proved to be completely impossible. We had nowhere near the money necessary to acquire the sort of house which we thought we should have. We slipped further and further down market until eventually we bought a top flat in

Brougham Place in Edinburgh. It had some advantages: it was a very spacious house and the people selling it to us had got into financial difficulties and left quite a lot of furniture to attract a purchaser. It had some disadvantages too: it was on a tram route and was fairly noisy—but we were happy. We were starting our lives in our own house. I remember we went into a shop in Edinburgh to buy a carpet; we were told that at the present intake of carpets into that store we would get one in 25 years' time. However, my mother had an old carpet which we turned upside down and painted on the bottom. We were perfectly pleased with that, and with various coupons that one could get at that time we managed to buy a three piece suite, a standard lamp and a mat which we put in front of the fire—we thought it was absolutely super.

Norma had got a clerical job in a brewery in Edinburgh, so financially we were able to handle our affairs reasonably comfortably. We had a lot of friends of similar age and similar style and we had a pretty good social life. The flat in Brougham Place had much more accommodation than we needed; it was really quite an extensive flat and we discovered that we could let a sitting room and a bedroom, and there was a very large cupboard which could be converted into a kitchen. We let these rooms to a retired bank inspector from India and his wife. This had many advantages other than the financial advantage that came from the bit of rent that this chap paid to us, because he was a very keen sportsman. He shot in the wintertime and fished in the summertime, and he was kind enough to provide us with hares and pheasants in the winter and with trout in the summer. His wife was still active as a dispenser in a chemist's shop in Edinburgh, so she was out all day and this chap used to do the cooking. As I have said, his kitchen was really a cupboard with no ventilation at all. This was all terrible really, when you come to think of it, because if he was cooking and if we had people coming we used to shut the door on the poor fellow, and all you could see was steam coming from round the sides and underneath the door while he made his meal in this unventilated cupboard. Of course at this time rationing was more severe than it had been during the war; everything was very scarce, so his contributions in the way of bits and pieces of game and fish were more than welcome to help us with our feeding.

In May 1949 our first child, John, was born, another joyous occasion for us. However, this was tempered slightly by the fact that very shortly afterwards my contract as a lecturer at Leith Nautical College was about to run out and I had to think about returning to sea. The thought of leaving my wife with this new baby was really pretty appalling. Before we were married we had discussed this and we had agreed that I would go to sea and knew it would be horrible for both of us; when we faced the eventual possibility of it happening it was even more horrible than we had imagined.

I had to decide what sort of ships I wanted to serve in; one of the things that made up my mind for me as the fact that Shell paid £50 a year extra, for people who had an Extra Master certificate. Fifty pounds a year in those days was quite an addition to one's salary; it seemed to me that if they were going to pay this they must have some good reason so I thought I would give this a whirl. I decided to join the then Anglo-Saxon Petroleum Company which was the marine part of the Shell worldwide empire.

I made my first voyage in a Shell tanker and went to Mina'al Ahmadi where we loaded a cargo of crude oil, which was brought back to the port of Heysham and there my wife, brave girl that she is, joined me with our young son, John. I remember the baby being handed up by some burly chaps from a tug which had come off to the ship to bring the wives out. We spent the time in Heysham together until I had a message from the Shell office in London, to the effect that I was to come to the London office for some discussions. I didn't know what they might be, but I left that first ship. I remember there was a very long jetty in Heysham; my wife and I were walking down this jetty with the baby in a carrycot and under the mattress of the carrycot were quite a number of flat fifty tins of cigarettes. To our horror, walking along this jetty which was the best part of a mile long, we saw a large number of customs officers and it would have been very bad news if they had discovered that these flat fifties were lying underneath the baby's mattress in this carrycot. However, we walked up to these customs officers with cheerful expressions on our faces and they giggled and cooed and poked the baby and off we went.

CHAPTER TEN

Borneo

When we got back to our home in Edinburgh, about the end of 1949, there was a letter from Shell to the effect that they wanted me to come down to London for some discussions, and they were kind enough to allow me to bring my wife and baby with me. We were accommodated in a boarding house in Bromley in Kent. We spent quite a few days there, where it was explained to me that what they wanted was somebody to assist one of their senior superintendents in a survey in Borneo. The purpose of the survey was to find a terminal for tanker operations associated with a refinery which the company were proposing to build in the north part of British Borneo.

This had some exciting prospects as far as I was concerned; it was going to be a very interesting job for me. However, it was absolutely appalling as far as my wife and our life were concerned, because we had discovered by this time that Norma was pregnant with our second child and the thought of my going away and leaving her was absolutely horrific. This commission to north Borneo was completely open-ended in terms of time, and at that time fleet people were supposed to be prepared to spend two years on any stretch abroad. The thought of leaving my wife with one baby and another to be born whilst I was away was really awful. She put the bravest possible face on it, but both of us felt absolutely terrible. We came home to Edinburgh for a spot of leave and clung together, with this awful prospect of my going away for an unlimited period of time, leaving my wife to be delivered of our second child.

I think the separations that followed were always easier for me than they were for Norma, because I had exciting things to do and I was tremendously involved with what I had to do, whereas she had to sit at home with tiny children, without her husband. But she showed enormous character and bravery; I am sure that many wives would have moaned and made their husband's life miserable. She bore all her difficulties with tremendous fortitude and I can't be more proud of her.

The senior superintendent that I was to assist in this hydrographic survey in North Borneo was a chap called John T. Kirk. Before accepting the commission from Shell to be in charge of this survey in Borneo,

Captain Kirk had advised the company that he had applied for a post in the Irish government in their marine offices as a marine surveyor. Whether the company didn't think he would be offered or accept the job I really don't know, but in any case the company still wished him to lead the expedition to north Borneo. He was also an Extra Master Mariner and I think that I was aware at this time that having this extra certificate had made it possible for me to be selected as his assistant. In due time we both turned up at London airport to go off to Singapore and we were due to fly in a Constellation, I remember. It was my first experience of long distance flying, and long distance flying in those days really was very pleasurable. I well remember flying over Europe, in the wintertime, between Mont Blanc and the Matterhorn with beautiful Alpine scenery all around. We made Rome in time for lunch. In those days the aircraft took a very long time to refuel and get into shape for the next part of the flight, so having had our lunch on the ground in Rome we were taken in a bus around the antiquities of the ancient city of Rome. The conductor of this bus was a man who was absolutely fascinated by Rome and he made everything come alive; to this day I have a great fascination for Rome, largely attributable, I think, to this BOAC man's enthusiasm for his subject.

In due time, in the late afternoon, we took off for the second part of the voyage which was to fly to Cairo. In those days the aircraft didn't fly at night and we landed at Cairo in time for an evening meal. I remember we were accommodated at the Anapolis Palace Hotel in an outlying district. It was a very good hotel and I can remember thinking what a splendid way this was to travel. The following day we took off and flew to Karachi, where we had another overnight stop. In those days you had two kinds of baggage in the aircraft: you had your main baggage and you had an overnight bag, which was available for these overnight stops. In Karachi I remember we were accommodated in the British Airways Hotel. The following day we took off from Karachi and flew to Singapore. There was no great hurry about it and there was no serious problem with time change; it was a very pleasant way of travelling.

In those days the marine side of the Shell organisation had a very substantial office in Singapore; they looked after the Eastern activities of the Shell fleet of ships. We had a lot of discussion with the Singapore office as to what our communications were going to be with them and with London. In due time we took passage by tanker from Singapore to the oil loading point in Borneo, loading from sea lines from Miri. Miri had been the centre of Shell's oil operations in Borneo before the war, but the northern fields which had been discovered immediately before the war were in Seria. This lay in Brunei further up the coast of north Borneo and it was there that the main offices of the oilfields were situated. We went from Miri to Seria and had very extensive briefing discussions with the management in the Seria oilfield as to what our duties were going to be, what was going to be available to us and how we were going to conduct our operations.

The coast of Borneo in those days was really very interesting. There weren't an enormous number of European people and in a very short time everybody knew everybody else. We travelled from Miri to Seria in a jeep and the roads were rather appalling. We had to cross a pretty substantial river, the River Baram, on the way, on a very antiquated ferry that went regularly across the river. The Seria oilfields had been occupied by the Japanese during the war. The Japanese had done a considerable amount of damage before they left, not only to the oilfields but also to the housing and other things. The housing had been replaced by temporary accommodation which just amounted to bungalows made out of woven palm leaves, and all the oilfield staff were accommodated in this manner. We, on the other hand, lived in old wooden bungalows which had been built before the war and had been used by the Japanese. They were in pretty shocking condition, but our sleeping accommodation was perfectly adequate. We had to sleep under mosquito nets; the mosquitoes were very prevalent, and we fed in communal messes with all the young unmarried fellows. Strangely enough, one of the geologists was the fellow I had pulled out of the water in the Mediterranean, who came from Aberdeen.

About the second week or so after our arrival in Borneo, Captain Kirk learned that he had been offered the job that he had applied for in Ireland and he accepted it. This gave the company quite a lot of problems and they decided that he would be replaced by one of the marine superintendents from Singapore, Captain Broom. He was a very pleasant chap to work for and with, but he really didn't have much knowledge of hydrographic surveying or any of the other work that we were supposed to be doing, so I think he felt rather at some disadvantage. So, to a very large extent I was left on my own to organise affairs and to get things done in any way that I thought appropriate.

Another chap who did have quite a lot of hydrographic survey experience, a Dutchman called Den Hollander, joined the party. I was then given a small ship and a fairly substantial launch to conduct our hydrographic survey of Brunei bay. The ship I was given for the survey was called *Pikau*; she was a converted LCT. The launch that we had was called *Perling*. Our first task was to make a chart of Brunei bay. The site was selected for the proposed refinery, the purpose of which was to refine

A selection of photographs from the author's family album.

Cadet Dickson is ready for pirates in the eastern seas.

The author with his mandolin in the cadet band during the dog watches.

Officers from the Northern Patrol, after bringing neutral ships into Kirkwall, 1939.

Promoted to Sub-lieutenant, 1940.

The family.

HMS *Relentless*. The author stood by the building of this ship at John Brown's shipyard, 1942.

Accelerated promotion to
Lieutenant, 1942.

On appointment as
First-lieutenant, HMS *Relentless*.

The author receives the Institute of Navigation medal from Admiral Irvine for his work on channel routeing.

Norma, after launching MV *Gertrude Maersk* in Oslo Fjord in ice and snow.

The author on election to the board of Shell International Marine Ltd.

Visit to Mashhour Ahmed Mashhour, chairman of the Suez Canal Authority, 1971.

A recent photograph of the author with a lightkeeper and Commander John
Mackay, Chief Executive of the Northern Lights Board.

Last sea voyage with the Northern Lights Board.

the oil from the Borneo oilfields and send it around the whole of the Shell distribution area of the Far East at that time. The site that had been selected was on an island called Mouara Island. 'Moura', we learned, is the Malay for bar, and Mouara Island was, in fact, an old sand bar which was standing about two feet above water. The assumption was that the ships that would come in to load refined oil from this refinery would be ships of around 20,000 tonne dead weight, drawing some 30 feet of water. There was no channel that would allow entry or departure of ships of that weight, but we had to find the best channel we could, and thereafter consideration would be given to the desirability or otherwise of dredging to see whether adequate depth could be provided for these ships fully laden.

So, our first task really was to draw up a blank Mercator chart of Brunei bay. We then decided that we would have to put out a series of floating beacons, to allow us to fix accurately the lines of soundings on this chart over the area that was going to be used as a channel into the proposed refinery. We made beacons out of oil drums, and anchored the beacons in suitable positions around the area of the bay to be surveyed. We had the assistance of surveyors from the oilfield to fix the positions of our beacons on the chart we had made. Then the real hydrographic work started. We had quite efficient echo sounding equipment, and I thought we could use the *Pikau* to run lines of soundings. She, however, proved to be far too difficult to manoeuvre so we had to use *Perling*. The crews of both *Pikau* and *Perling* spoke no English so I had to learn Malay. Fortunately Malay is a fairly easy language to learn, and I found that through speaking it all day, every day, I became sufficiently proficient very quickly.

There were a lot of small villages around the coast of Brunei Bay and we found that the people there were very willing to help. We could employ them quite easily to do any jobs that we wanted done and pay them whatever was the going rate, which seemed to be to be very modest indeed. This meant that we got to know a lot of the local people and on my first contacts with them, I thought they were rather backward. I soon found out that the boot could very easily be on the other foot; these Malays were just as intelligent as I was, perhaps more so, and they had the advantage of knowing exactly what was what in that part of the world, which I didn't.

My first exposure to the difference between my concept of the way things should be and theirs came when we wanted to employ them to do some particular job. I would say 'Right chaps, we'll start at eight in the morning and we'll finish at five in the afternoon, and these are the hours you will work.' Well, they just looked at me in blank astonishment; this was quite foreign to any thoughts that they had ever had about doing any job at all. Their response was 'No, no, no, no, no. That's not how we would like to approach this: you tell us what we have to do and we will do it and that'll be that. If it takes a long time then we'll get paid a lot and if it takes a short time then we won't get paid as much, but all this stuff about starting at some time in the morning and finishing at a set time in the evening is just not on. We like to work when we want to work, and we will work, but we won't work if we don't want to work.' That was that, and that was how it was. Eventually I got to believing that their way was entirely sensible.

The people who lived in the various small villages around that area of Borneo were leading a very happy life. They had no great difficulty in finding food and if they wanted to build a house they could do so in virtually no time at all. The common way of dealing with things was that if somebody wanted a house, all his chums from the village would come, and in a few days they would have the house built for him, so it presented no problem at all. However, they had to have clothing and there were things that they esteemed; they were very fond of knives and they needed cloth. They were very keen on electric torches. In order to buy these they had to deal with the Chinese towkies who went round the various villages—they could buy whatever they wanted from them. About the only cash crop they had was crocodile skins; crocodiles were plentiful in the rivers of Borneo, and very dangerous sea crocodiles were very common in the estuaries. They had all sorts of ways of catching these crocodiles. One method I particularly admired was to take a bamboo, bend it round, stick the two pointed ends of the bamboo into a piece of meat, then throw it into the river. The old crocodile in due time would swallow the meat and start digesting it; when he got through part of his digestion the bamboo would spring apart and puncture him in both sides, until eventually he would come to the surface and they could catch and skin him. When I got to know the local Malays, I thought it would be sensible to suggest to them that they could make quite a lot of money by selling fish to the oilfield people living 80 miles down the coast at Seria. At that time, fish was being flown from Australia up to the island of Labuan and from there it was taken to the oilfield stores in Seria. Brunei Bay was absolutely teeming with fish, and the fishermen used to go out in their praus and catch whatever fish they wanted. So when I knew them well enough I said 'Look, I can help you to run a profitable business here. What we'll do is we'll either use my launch or get another launch and put a freezer into it, you can go fishing and we will take the fish down and sell it in the oilfields in Seria.' They were kind enough to thank me for this idea, and said that they had already thought about that, but the thing was that although they very much liked fishing, they wouldn't want to do it every day!

The way things were arranged in the village, there were three logs arranged in an open ended rectangle. The people from the village would come and sit down on these logs, and any suggestion anyone wished to make would be considered and accepted or rejected by the assembled company. They made it very clear to me that any suggestion that fishing would become a way of life would have absolutely no support.

Another thing that I thought was very interesting was that, although they were basically, I suppose, hunter/gatherer communities, they did grow a certain amount of rice. The first thing they did when they came to harvest the rice was to make some rice beer; everybody had a jolly good time, and that was a real opening to what you might say was the local harvest.

Another example I had of the local way of doing things was when we had to gather accurate tidal information for the proposed channel, because we would have to make use of whatever tide would be available to get the maximum amount of depth we could in the channels. I had, before leaving London, taken some instruction from the Admiralty as to how one did a tidal survey. The essential information to make the calculation to be able to predict tides for a given area was gleaned by observing the height of the tide over a 24-hour period, hour by hour, for at least one tidal month. I felt that it would be necessary to do this in three different points around the coast of Brunei Bay. I consulted with my Malays in the ship as to how we might employ people to do this; after some discussion the consensus was that it wouldn't be too difficult. None of the men we planned to employ could read or write, but that didn't matter too much because all we would do would be to take alarm clocks, which we could get from the oilfield, and teach them how the hour hand moved around the clock. We would then set up a station with three men so that they could keep watch during the 24 hours and record the height of the tide every hour. We would put tide poles down into the water marked off in feet and inches, so they could determine what was written on the pole and write that in the book to be provided. They wouldn't need to know what they were writing; all they would have to do was to record exactly what the tide pole said for each hour.

I set up these three stations and provided the three Malays in each one with enough food to last for a week, and I thought it would be a good idea to go and have a look at them after a week to see how they were getting on. My Malays in the ship said, 'Oh no, I don't think we should leave them a week. I think we should go and see them', I think this was after about two days. I said, 'Oh no, they've got plenty of provisions', but they insisted that we should go and see them. I thought that I had better follow the local advice, so off we went. Sure enough, when we got to the first station and asked them how they were getting on, they said that everything was going very well but they had run out of food. I asked what they meant, saying they had run out of food, as they had been provisioned for a week. They said they had a lot of friends who came to see them, and they had eaten all the food. What had happened was that they thought this was a bonanza; the first thing they had done was to find any people they could and invite them round and they had just eaten up everything they had. From this it was clear that the tidal observation business was going to take a lot more of my time than I had thought. In due time I found out how to get a working system, we did get accurate observations which allowed us to do the necessary calculations and produce tide tables for the area.

The hydrographic survey of the area was a very arduous and time-consuming operation. We had put out a floating triangulation with our beacons so that we could cover the area of the proposed channel adequately. The Dutchman and I could take horizontal sexton angles on this floating triangulation, and we ran lines of soundings more or less from dawn until dusk. Then we sat on the deck of the *Pikau* and applied whatever correction had to be made to the soundings to allow for the height of the tide at the time the soundings had been taken; we inked the soundings in on the chart, a fairly laborious process.

However it wasn't all work and no play; I am a very keen fisherman, and always have been, and the Malays in the ship and I used to go fishing sometimes quite late into the night. In Brunei Bay we caught quite a lot of very edible fish. We had a super Chinese cook on the ship. I don't know how he managed to produce the meals he did, because the cooking facilities were absolutely appalling, but he made an oven for himself and managed to conjure up some very good food indeed.

My Malay crew taught me how to fish for crabs and various flat fish in the shallow water on the sand, close by the island which was going to be the site of this proposed refinery. What we did was we had very large bamboos which were hollowed out and filled with stuff like cotton wool; into these we poured paraffin which was lit to make a torch. We had long bamboo spears and we used to go around on this sand spit spearing crabs and flat fish. The crabs were absolutely excellent eating; some of the fish weren't quite so good, though. One of the things that slightly worried me was that my white feet looked like crabs in this rather dim light; on more than one occasion the fishermen came quite close to trying to stab my feet!

Shell had a consultant who was in overall charge of the work we were doing. His name was Dr Ringers; he had been a member of the government in Holland, and was a professor of Delft University. He was a very distinguished civil engineer and a very remarkable gentleman in many ways. I had to go and meet him in Labuan, which was our base, to take him round some of the work which we had done to date and get his guidance as to how we were to conduct the rest of our affairs. I remember my first meeting with him. It was a very hot day; Labuan is a typical tropical island and the climate of north Borneo is a typical tropical climate—fairly moist and very hot all the time. To my surprise, here was this gentleman, Dr Ringers, in quite a heavy tweed suit, with a waistcoat and a watch chain stretched across the front of his waistcoat. As far as I could tell, he was giving absolutely no thought at all to the climate, and was wearing a black homburg hat. It would have been a very suitable garb for Amsterdam or the Hague but it was pretty unusual in Labuan. I found him a very charming gentleman and, fortunately, he seemed to think that I was doing a fairly reasonable job. He sent a report to London to that effect, which I imagine did me quite a lot of good in my progress in the marine side of the Shell organisation.

Dr Ringers was very interested in the possibilities that would exist if dredging had to be done in the channel into this proposed refinery site. To that end, he wanted us to conduct a lot of surveys of silt transportation in the various rivers feeding into Brunei Bay. This involved us taking the *Perling* up the various rivers quite a long way. It was most fascinating; we met some interesting tribesmen coming down from the hills.

I mentioned earlier that Mouara Island, which was the preferred potential site for the refinery, was a sandbank in the entrance to the Brunei river. Dr Ringers was beginning to think that this sandbank really wouldn't be a very suitable site for the heavy equipment that would be necessary to build the refinery. This view was later to be borne out by some civil engineers who came out from the office in the Hague. They immediately came to the conclusion that Mouara Island would need to be piled all round and filled and made much more secure before the refinery could be built on it. So Dr Ringers asked me to look at two other locations for the possible site of the refinery, one was an island—more a peninsula than an island, a rather hilly peninsula called Bukit Sari. When I told my crew that I was going to have a look at this peninsula, they seemed rather uneasy. When I asked them what the trouble was, they said that it was full of very bad spirits. This didn't make any impression on me at all, of course, because I wasn't really interested in the local spirits. However, on the first approach I made to land to have a look at the coast line on the island it did seem a very forbidding place. I wasn't at all concerned about the spirits, but I was concerned about the nasty swell which sometimes came into Brunei Bay from the China Sea. This would bash against the heavy rocks surrounding the coast of this island, and would make landing very difficult. On the particular day that I decided that I would have a walk around the shore of the island, it was quite impossible to land. I decided to anchor the ship about half a mile off the island, although the crew were not at all happy.

By this time in the survey operations, my Dutch colleague had left and had been replaced by a young Australian third officer from the fleet who had been sent to give me a hand. He was a very good man; he and I used to sleep on the open deck of the LCT because the cabin that we had was pretty hot and stuffy. One day, in the early hours of the morning, I suppose it must have been two o'clock or so, I heard the most terrible commotion. People were shouting and screaming on the main deck of the ship, so I went along to have a look to see what it was about, and found the crew in a state of high excitement. As far as I could gather, one of the crew believed that he had just saved the ship from severe trouble, because the ship had been boarded by an adat, a dreadful spirit from this island. This man, with great bravery, had taken the spirit by the arm, and he described the person—who obviously had a human form—as having long, grey hair and bright, fiery eyes. He took this frightening spirit, with great bravery, to the side of the ship and pushed him over into the sea. The crew were all busy congratulating him on his bravery and making it clear to me that they didn't wish to remain there any longer. I came to the conclusion that it would probably be sensible to move the ship further out into the middle of the bay. I imagine the logical explanation of this incident was that the man had had a dream; he had then woken up and told people what had happened. However, it was clear to me that the crew were quite prepared to believe his story as he told it.

There were certainly some very strange things on the coast of Borneo. There was an island further north of Brunei Bay called Mangallan Island. The geologists in the oilfield were anxious to do some survey work on this island, in connection with the possibility of extending the Seria oilfield and eventual drilling in the sea further north from where there had been drilling at that time. I remember the geologists telling me they had had a lot of trouble getting local assistants to explore this island, because there was a belief that there was an evil spirit attached to a ship's anchor which was on the island. These geologists, after surveying most of the island, eventually came across this anchor, much to the horror of their local assistants. I understand the anchor was positioned more or less in the middle of this relatively small island; it did seem very strange that an anchor from a ship could be situated so far from the sea. Apparently, the anchor was usually festooned with all sorts of feathers, pieces of cloth and branches, and was more or less a place of worship for the local people on the island.

Quite naturally, during all this period I was carrying on a weekly correspondence with my wife and learning how our son John was coming along. I was therefore very interested in the local children, and was fascinated by the fact that in the communities around Brunei Bay, the parents had the most wonderful relationship with their children. They were very caring people; they seemed to have no problem in matters of discipline which, in our society, do arise from time to time with children. I suppose the children couldn't really misbehave, because there was nothing to break and they were allowed to play pretty much as they liked. I remember that one of the crew of the LCT had a child die whilst we were on the survey; when I tried to show him sympathy he just laughed and said, 'Buleh bekin lagi', which is Malay for 'Can make more'. As I have said, they were caring and loving parents, but the life and death of children didn't seem to mean the same to these people as it did to us.

About this time, war had broken out in Korea. In the crew of *Pikau* there was one chap who was a Dyak; he came from one of the longhouses up the River Baram. He very kindly said that if Borneo were again to be invaded by hostile people, he would be very happy to take me up to his longhouse, where I could live until the trouble was over. He was obviously thinking of what had happened during World War II, when the Japanese had invaded Borneo, and one or two of the Europeans then resident in Borneo had been given hospitality in the Dyak longhouses during the occupation. The Dyak was, very kindly, imagining that this same kind of thing might happen again. The Eastern people generally were quite amazed by the collapse of European domination in the Far East during the Japanese part of World War II. Obviously, this chap thought the same might happen again with the Chinese.

Around this time, Dr Ringers was living in the oil camp in the oilfield in Seria. He wanted me to come down from time to time and report on my progress in the survey in Brunei Bay. He also wanted me to set up some observations off the coast of Seria, to prepare for eventual offshore drilling. This meant travelling from the town of Brunei down to the oilfield of Seria, which was a very interesting journey. At that time, there was no road, so we had to travel down the beach in an American jeep. There were quite a number of jeeps, which had been left by the American troops after the capture of Borneo from the Japanese forces at the end of the war. These jeeps were extraordinary vehicles; if you were careful you could drive them with reasonable confidence along the beach. However, every now and again, you could hit a patch of soft sand and the jeep would sink axle deep into the sand. There were always Dyaks moving one way or another along the beach—the distance from Brunei to Seria was, I suppose, the best part of 80 miles, so the Dyaks were always looking for a lift. The Dyaks always carried parangs with them; no Dyak would ever be seen out in the the open without his parang. The trick was to pick up a couple of Dyak hitchhikers as soon as possible; if the vehicle got stuck these chaps would disappear and come back, having cut palm fronds with the parangs; these were most effective in providing escape from soft sand on the beach.

Dr Ringers had been asked to advise the local company on two matters; firstly, the erosion of the coast of Seria due to wave action from the North China Sea, and secondly, the possibility of eventual drilling in the sea off the coast of Seria. He asked me to undertake wave observations; we did this by putting an observation hut up on an oil derrick, on a platform which had been built at the end of a walkway, about half a mile out into the sea. We measured the direction of the incoming waves by a theodilite with a bar across it; the bar was simply lined up on the line of the waves and recorded. These recordings were made every hour, and once again I used the local chaps on a sort of three-man watch system, which worked out quite well.

By this time, the company had come to the conclusion that having a refinery up in Brunei Bay was not such a good idea. The limitation of ship size was going to be quite serious, and the Dutch civil engineers had concluded that Mouara Island was a hopeless place to try and locate the heavy equipment necessary for an oil refinery. So, all the work we had done in Brunei Bay had been for no purpose; the only good that came of it was that the Admiralty accepted all my work in the hydrographic soundings of the Bay, as well as the tidal work. Although I was pleased about this, it was very little recompense. I had been hoping that, at the end of this fairly long stint, I would be sent home for discussions about what had taken place; in the event, that was not to be, and I was sent back to Singapore to join one of the ships. This was terrible news as far as my wife was concerned—I hated it too—but she had just delivered our second child, a daughter, and she was expecting me to come home and help her with our small child and the new baby. That was not to be; she was dismayed when she received a telegram to the effect that I was going to stay out east for quite a while longer.

The Korean war had given the Navy a lot to think about, and it was decided that reserve officers of my rank and seniority—I was at that time a lieutenant commander—with destroyer experience should be put through a destroyer command course, so I was brought home to undertake this training. I took passage back to the UK in one of the P & O ships, which was quite an experience. It took 26 days to go from Singapore to Tilbury, via Penang, Colombo, Aden, then through the canal and through the Mediterranean. It was a very pleasant voyage home, the only time I had ever spent in a passenger ship, and it really was quite a delightful life. We had a good bridge school and super meals; it was very relaxing and pleasant.

The naval training was also very pleasant; I was able to take my wife and the two small children, and we lived in a boarding house in Southsea. The courses were nearly all in Portsmouth and it lasted about six weeks as I remember. I don't really think that I learned very much on these courses; most of what we were taught I had already been fairly familiar with in HMS *Relentless*. One thing which sticks in my mind about the course was that we were sent to the naval detention centre in Portsmouth for a day. The detention centre was run on exactly the same lines as HM prisons, and it made a deep impression on me. I have never been entirely happy about prisons; it has always seemed to me that a large proportion of the prison population are not vicious wicked people, but simply misfits in society. My experience of the naval prison just confirmed the general ideas I had. The people running the prison didn't particularly impress me; they were almost sadistic, making people do things like dig holes and then fill them in again.

At the end of my naval course I went back to the fleet. I was taking a ship through the Suez Canal when a message came from the company that again they wanted me to come back to the London office, so I was relieved in the Suez Canal in Egypt. I later had quite a lot to do with the Egyptians and the Suez Canal, and I found the Egyptians quite delightful people. However, at this time General Nageeb had taken over in Egypt, and there was very strong anti-British feeling in Egypt. I was accommodated in a hotel in Port Said waiting for another Shell ship, on which I was to take passage back to London to see what the company wanted of me. I had to report to the Egyptian police every day, which was pretty unpleasant. The chap in charge of the police station in Port Said was a very unpleasant young Egyptian soldier; when I was ushered into his office, he would take out an automatic which he would lay on the desk in front of him, and ask me all sorts of questions about what I was doing, where I was going and who I was seeing. He never did me any harm, but it was rather unpleasant.

In due course I joined a Shell tanker as a passenger going back to the United Kingdom. Eventually, I arrived at the head office in London, where it was explained to me that the company wanted me to go out to Singapore to do a tidal survey of the island of Pulau Bukum. Pulau Bukum, an island lying in the Singapore Strait, was the base for the distribution of Shell products all over the Far East. The company wanted to build two more jetties; I think there were already six jetties, and they wanted to build these other two at the northern end of the island. The local pilots had said that it was impossible to berth ships there, because the tides were so completely unpredictable. Sometimes they ran one way and sometimes they ran another, and berthing ships there would be very hazardous. So I was asked to undertake a tidal survey, to see whether we could predict the tides, so that ships would be able to berth on the new jetties to be constructed on the north end of the island.

I flew out to Singapore and had meetings in the Shell marine offices there. It was agreed that we would commission a Danish civil engineer to assist in these surveys. He was a very pleasant and interesting chap. His office was quite a long way out from Singapore, and one day he asked if I would like to come out to his office and spend the day with him, so that we could talk about how we would approach this survey and how we were going to analyse the results, and so on. He asked if I liked Chinese food and I said I loved it, and he said there was a little Chinese place nearby where we could have our lunch. Well, I do like Chinese food, but I did not like the Chinese food we had on that particular occasion. It really wasn't a restaurant, it was a little feeding place where the local Chinese had their meals—our meal consisted of a heap of rice with a rather dubious few cabbage leaves on top, and a rather horrible bit of meat. It was nothing at all like the magnificent meals one could have in the high class Chinese restaurants in the town of Singapore.

This Danish civil engineer was a very clever man; he and I decided we would have to get raw tidal information over a month, that being a full tidal period. What we did was to make tide poles which would float vertically in the water to the draught of the ships that would use the jetties. We used four of these tide poles in line on the tide, and set up theodolite stations on the island, so that the tide poles could be fixed in position by cross bearings from the theodolites, taken, say, every five minutes. So we had to man the stations ashore with people from the civil engineers office and with one or two young officers from the fleet, who were ashore awaiting appointments to ships from the Singapore office.

We set the tide poles using three small Chinese junks, which we got to tow the tide poles up to a position at the end of the island and release them into the water so that they floated down on the tide. They were then observed from the shore station so that all the raw data could be taken to the civil engineer's office in Singapore to be plotted out so that we could analyse it. It was the Danish civil engineer who really discovered the reason why the tide suddenly changed direction. He realised that what was happening was that the main tide flowing through the Singapore Strait flowed past the island of Pulau Bukum which lay at an angle across the main tidal flow. When the main tidal current reached a critical velocity—which was just over one knot—it produced an eddy behind the island, so that the tides suddenly changed direction and flowed the opposite way. This solved the problem and enabled the tide to be predicted; thereafter, it was necessary to avoid berthing ships at the time when the tide reached the critical velocity of roughly one knot. We were able to build the jetties, task was successfully completed.

CHAPTER ELEVEN

Assistant Marine Superintendent

I n the early 1950s, the company decided I should be brought ashore
permanently as an assistant marine superintendent. This was a major
change in our lives as it meant that from then on, I would be permanently
based in London—or that was the presumption at the time—so my wife
and I were accommodated in a hotel in the south of London. We began
to look for a house, and chose a house in Wallington, Surrey, so we sold
the house in Scotland so we could buy it.

The company decided that I should have some formal training in
hydrographic surveying, because I had done quite a number of
hydrographic surveying jobs for them. To this effect, they sought the
Admiralty's agreement to my joining one of the naval hydrographic ships.
The Admiralty agreed to this, and I was sent to join HMS *Cook* under
the command of a very well known naval surveyor, Captain Buck Baker.

I joined the ship in the Western Isles and we did a survey of a loch
south of Stornoway, which was very interesting and pleasant. One of the
other officers in the ship was a very keen trout fisherman; he and I used
to land in the loch we were surveying and go inland a bit and fish the
trout lochs, with great success. After that, the ship went down to do a
survey in the Severn estuary. This was very interesting, since the tides in
the Severn estuary are higher than anywhere else in the United Kingdom.
In fact, at the top of the estuary there can be a spring tide of around forty
feet, which is quite incredible.

Captain Baker was a very interesting man. When I joined the ship, I
was joining as a civilian in training—nothing to do with my naval
background—but he immediately said to me, 'You're an RNR officer, are
you not?' and I said I was. So he said that, from now on, I should wear
my uniform on the ship as he didn't want anyone walking around his ship
with a felt hat on. I did, in fact, wear my uniform on the ship; Captain
Baker wanted me to act in every way as an officer of the ship, and I used
to keep watch and do all sorts of things, which I enjoyed very much.

Captain Baker's passion was grandfather clocks, of which he had quite
a number in his cabin in HMS *Cook*. He couldn't have them going at
sea, since any movement of the ship would upset the pendulums of the

clocks, but as soon as we got into harbour he used to unleash all the pendulums. At these times, his cabin was just a cacophony of ticking of all these old grandfather clocks.

I enjoyed my time in HMS *Cook*, and I've always regarded the hydrographic division of the Royal Navy as being very hardworking. The surveyors often spent all day in boats running lines of soundings; then they would spend quite a bit of time after dinner inking in their surveys onto the fair charts, which are sent in due time to the printing department of the hydrographic part of the Navy. But, as far as I was concerned, here again I was being trained for something that I had already done, and as far as I remember, I did very little hydrographic surveying for the company after this training in HMS *Cook*.

One of the early jobs that I was given having come ashore as an assistant marine superintendent was to represent Shell's interests in a joint company venture to set up a refinery in southern Ireland. It had been decided that the refinery would be built in Cork; the site chosen for the jetty for crude tankers coming in to discharge crude for refining in the Irish refinery was in the outer part of the harbour. I was very concerned about this, because it seemed to me that the part of the harbour that had been chosen for the jetty would be subject to serious swell coming in from the south-west and the berth would be unsafe. So it was agreed that a team of marine people representing the companies involved in the refinery project should look around the coast of Ireland to see if there was a more suitable site for the refinery. The leading company was Esso; there was an Esso man in charge of the investigation. We had a Humber Pullman motorcar, I remember, and the idea was to go around Ireland and look at all the possibilities. I remember the harbour master of Dublin received us and produced, I think, five bottles of Irish whiskey, saying, 'Gentlemen, the first thing we have to decide is which of these you like the best!' There was an Esso man, a BP man, a Caltext man, and myself representing Shell, and by the time we sorted out who liked which whiskey we'd had a fairly hilarious meeting. Nevertheless, it was quite obvious that Dublin couldn't accommodate the sort of ships we would need for the refinery, so it was immediately discounted as a possibility.

We then went over to Shannon, which was a marvellous site from a marine point of view. Apparently, however, it was not going to be at all satisfactory for the distribution of products, so eventually we came back to Cork. Although, by then, everyone agreed that I was right in assuming the original site for the jetty in the outer part of the harbour would be too dangerous, it was agreed that we could get a convenient berth in the inner harbour in Cork. All the representatives of the various companies came to the conclusion that this was the right site—at a rather late hour, in a pub in the vicinity of the proposed jetty site. The Esso chap in charge of the team said we had better get an option on this land; I thought this was very peculiar, because it was quite a late hour. However, we got into our big Humber Pullman motorcar and drove into the town of Cork, where this chap knew a lawyer, and with the man who owned the land we knocked the lawyer up. It seemed to be quite a reasonable thing to do in southern Ireland; I can't think of anywhere else in the world where you could do that. This chap seemed to be quite happy to be woken up; his wife made us some tea and sandwiches, and in no time we had an option on the land. In due time, the refinery was built, and it was very successful.

About this time, Shell were looking at the employment of much larger tankers to carry refined products to various marketing installations around the world. I was sent out to the Caribbean to survey the various ports being supplied in the islands, to see whether larger ships could be employed to deliver products to these island installations. At the same time, I was asked to look into the question of offshore drilling off the coast of Trinidad. My old mentor, Dr Ringers, had been asked by the company to advise on how the offshore drilling equipment could be most conveniently built in Trinidad.

The depots in the islands of Jamaica, Haiti, Dominican Republic and San Juan were administered from Kingston, Jamaica, and I had to make a report there about the tanker facilities in the depots in these islands. The depots in the Windward Islands and the Guyanas were administered from Trinidad, so I had to make another report there about the depots in these places.

The Trinidad Company were thinking of developing a depot in a place called Batika up the Esquibo River, and I was asked whether it would be possible to put large tankers up this river to supply the depot. To this end, we chartered a small aircraft in Georgetown in British Guyana. An engineer from the company, and myself, were due to take off in this little Gruman Goose aircraft fairly early in the morning. In fact, we got to the little place where the aircraft was sited, on the bank of the river, just before dawn on a really horrible morning. I remember we went into the shed where all the equipment for the aircraft was kept, and there was a chap with a long pointed cap and a whole lot of pencils and spectacles and various other items in his pocket—I can see him yet. He was obviously suffering a severe hangover, and I thought he must be the chap who removed the chocks from the aircraft—but, to my horror, I discovered he was the pilot, a chap called Harry Witt. However, I was assured that he was a very good bush pilot and that he had a very long record of successful flying in his aircraft. In due time, the aircraft was sitting on a very steep bank of the river, with a chap holding a rope around a tree. We all got into the aircraft and Harry Witt, the pilot, got the fellow to let the turns of the rope slip on the tree. Gradually, the Gruman Goose, a little twin engined flying boat, was allowed to slip down into the river, and the rope was unhooked from the tail of the aircraft, Harry Witt, without worrying about checking magnetos or any of the normal things one did in aircraft in those days, just put both engines into full throttle and belted the plane out into the middle of the river in pouring rain and very limited visibility, which I thought was shocking. However, we came to no harm and we got airborne; then Harry Witt asked what exactly we would like to see. I was stupid enough to say that I was interested in the turns of the Esquibo river, and that I wanted to fly right up the river to Batika, looking at the various bends in the river. That was a pretty silly thing to do, because there were huge tropical forest trees on either bank of the river, and Harry Witt decided that what we wanted was to fly the aircraft at practically zero height round these bends, in between the trees which was pretty hair-raising. However, everything went reasonably well and we eventually landed the plane at Batika. I came to the conclusion that we could get fairly large tankers up the river; however, the distribution people decided that distributing products from this little place was going to be awkward, so as far as I am aware, the depot was never built.

I found it very interesting visiting the various islands to the north of Trinidad; some of them had a very strict attitude to skin colour, while some of them had a relatively relaxed attitude, and some ignored skin colour completely. It was very strange and interesting to observe how the different islands had developed.

Before leaving on this trip I had visited our offices in the Hague; there it was explained to me how they proposed to put the offshore drilling platform up. The platform was to go into the Gulf of Paria off the shore of Trinidad using two barges of about 200 tonnes each. On top of these would be a top hamper which would carry, slung between the two barges, a jacket. This was effectively a bunch of tubes, which would be carried out to the site, lowered onto the seabed, and through these tubes piles would be driven to provide a platform on which the drilling machinery could be built. Dr Ringers had asked me for my opinion on whether to do this it would be necessary to build a harbour—which would be very expensive—or whether it could be done on the unprotected beach. I concluded that it could be done on the unprotected beach: all that was necessary was to build a wooden jetty out into the sea, so that the barges could be moored off the jetty with wires going out to the sea. Then the top hamper could be built on the barges, and eventually the jacket which was going to be taken out and lowered onto the seabed could be suspended on the top hamper between the two barges. I reported all this on my return to the office of the civil engineering people in the Hague.

In due time, I got a message from the production people to the effect that, as I had advised on how this could be done, I should now go and do it! This was going to be a fairly long stint in Trinidad; however, my wife and family had settled down quite happily in Wallington in Surrey and, although I was at this time theoretically shore-based in London, I seemed to be spending just as much time away from home as I had done when I was in the fleet. Again, I have to pay tribute to my wife, who never complained—I'm sure that she often felt lonely and deprived of her husband's company. Also, it seemed that if anything was ever going to go wrong with any of the children, it happened when I was away or just about to leave. However, brave girl that she is, she never complained at all, and I very much appreciate how she managed to cope with all the difficulties she had to suffer because of my absence.

The production company in Trinidad in 1954 had not really been doing very well, so that great hopes were staked on this offshore drilling operation which we were going to carry out. The geologists in the oilfield in Trinidad had carried out some seismological surveys, and had picked out what they thought was the best possible site. The whole operation really depended on a team of three of us: there was a civil engineer from the Hague—a chap called Langeveldt who became a very close friend of mine, and he and I did many a job together—one of the local civil engineers from the oilfield, a chap called Alcock; and myself. My responsibility was to help with the seagoing part of the operation, and the first job that we had to do was to build a small platform so that the civil engineers could conduct what were called Dutch cone tests. These tests gave them some knowledge as to how the piling operation would go when the jacket was finally taken out and piled onto the seabed. This meant that we had to drive some piles and construct a small platform on which a piece of civil engineering investigation could be sited. A cone-shaped rod down into the seabed and you could, with this equipment, measure the resistance to the cone as it travelled down through the various layers on the seabed.

I found my contact with the production side of the oil business strange, because their attitude to risk was quite different to the attitude to risk that I had always been used to in the shipping world. It is rather difficult to explain this, but in the shipping world one always attempts to take a no risk attitude to everything that one does. You never hazard your ship. It obviously doesn't always work out like that; ships do get lost, but the basic assumption is that you don't take any risks that can be avoided. Conversely, the production side of the oil industry is quite used to taking risks and hazarding their equipment, in circumstances which are quite different to the way that shipping people approach their problems. It is quite incredible to think of it now, but the total budget for the first well to be put out in the sea was $350,000 (US); I suppose with modern drilling in the North Sea you probably wouldn't be able to buy a drilling bit for that sort of money. Certainly, the company in Trinidad hadn't really been doing very well financially and they were very anxious to save money wherever they could. The result of this was that we had to take quite a lot of risks, which I suppose I was not used to doing. I remember we had moored the barges offshore as I had anticipated, and erected the structure on the barge, with a gallery across between the two barges on which the jacket was going to be supported. It was built, in fact, in situ, with the barges lying off the beach. I had laid out anchors to keep the barges in position, but we had to lift these heavy piles into position on the barges, to be towed out. We didn't have a crane that was powerful enough to lift the piles, so the chief engineer—who was a Yorkshireman and a chap who wasn't prone to spending money if he could help it—said, 'Well, what we will do is we'll make a crane for this job.' He had a drag line, which was effectively a crane jib, which was used for towing a bucket for excavation work; he said we would strengthen the jib of this thing by welding some additional steel onto it, and with the back weighted down we would be able to lift these piles into position.

Well, it really was quite terrible when I think of it. On one occasion the jib of this wretched crane came crashing down—fortunately nobody was hurt, but that was pure good fortune—when I think of the way in which safety and care of the workforce is looked at nowadays, what we did was quite appalling. However, as I say, we got away with it, and in due time the whole object of the exercise was completed and ready to be towed out to its location.

My prime responsibility in all this, of course, was to actually manoeuvre this wretched piece of equipment out onto the drilling site, and here again we were really quite short of adequate equipment. The tug we had, which was called the *Mallard*, was a small twin engine tug—I suppose on a good day when she was new, she had something like 400 hp—and I concluded that she really wasn't man enough for the job of towing this contraption out onto the site in the Gulf of Poria. The weather there is reasonably comfortable most of the time, but every now and again you could get struck by quite nasty squalls. I told the engineer who was in overall charge of all the operations that I wasn't really happy about this, so he said 'Well, in addition to the tug you've got a couple of launches. Why don't you use them as well?' So, with some misgivings I eventually agreed that we would tow this thing with the tug assisted by the two launches. The operation of getting the whole contraption off the moorings on the beach and underway to tow it to site was a fairly complicated manoeuvre. The whole of the assembled company in the oilfield came down to watch, and I am told, although I wasn't conscious of it at the time, that I was using some fairly strong nautical language while attempting to get this flotilla of ships into order and getting the thing underway and in tow down to the locality. I had previously laid out a system of buoys around the selected drilling position; the object of the exercise was to manoeuvre this jacket into position and then pick up the wires from the various mooring buoys, put them onto winches on the barges and then set the whole thing into position. It was quite a complicated operation, and unfortunately when we got down onto the site we were struck by quite a nasty squall which made life very difficult indeed. However, we did manage and we got the whole thing on site and properly moored up.

We had the chief geologist of the oilfield with us for this operation, because he, of course, was anxious to ensure that we were getting our equipment into exactly the right place—something which had to be managed with fairly simple maritime navigational aids. However, I regarded myself as being quite good at precise navigation, since I'd had a lot of experience of it, and in the event he was quite satisfied that we had got the equipment on the right location.

As I have said, when we did finally get moored up, we were hit by a pretty nasty squall. Coming back in the tug was very unpleasant indeed and the chief geologist was terribly seasick. His wife was extremely worried, and had gone to the manager of the oilfield and said that it was absolutely dreadful that her husband was out in this storm risking life and limb. In the event, we got back in the tug, although we were thoroughly soaked because even the wheelhouse in the tug was by no means watertight, and she was pitching into this very nasty head sea all the way back to the oilfield.

The company in Trinidad decided that, as I had been away from home for a fairly long time—I had been out there in my previous work to assess the possibilities of building the drilling jacket offshore, and I was now going to be out there for quite some time putting the equipment onto the site—it would be reasonable for my wife and children to be brought out to the oilfield. They very kindly arranged for this to be done, so my wife and children came out to Trinidad in a French liner called the *Antilles*. I am very glad to say that, after my wife's problems in looking after two small children with me away for these long periods, she really enjoyed coming out in the ship. Passenger ships in those days were beautiful, both outside and inside, and the *Antilles* was a very fine liner. The food and entertainment on board were really quite remarkable, and I am glad to say that my wife—deservedly—had a very nice time coming out to join me. I can remember my happiness when I went to meet the ship in Port of Spain and bringing my wife and two small children back down to the oilfield at Port Fortin.

As I have said, it was the local company who organised this; my marine bosses in London were not at all happy about it. They assumed, quite wrongly, that I had been instrumental in getting my wife to come out and join me, which was far from their ideas of how affairs should be conducted. They were still of a mind that their staff, if sent away on a job somewhere, would accord with the then fleet terms of employment. Officially, you could be sent away for any period of up to two years without leave, and without any thought of being joined by one's wife. I think that it could be that this was regarded as something of a black mark on my record in the marine side of the business in Shell. However, it made my stay and the rest of my time in Trinidad very happy. The family was accommodated in the rest house, which was very comfortable and rather like a small hotel. John, our eldest son, went to the local oilfield school.

I am glad to say that the well that was drilled on this first location was a great success. It brought in a considerable amount of oil, and was a boost to the fortunes of the local oil company in Trinidad. My presence was then no longer required there, and I was sent back to the London Marine Office of Shell.

Shell's marine business at this time was changing, and changing very dramatically, for two reasons. The first was that ever larger tankers were being built for the various jobs carrying petroleum products across the sea. The carriage of crude oil had previously been done in ships of around 12 to 18 thousand tonnes dead weight, but ships then called supertankers were being built, of 30 to 35 thousand tonnes dead weight. These, by standards of that time, were very big ships indeed. The other matter which gave rise to considerable change was that, whereas previously refined products—that is, the result of refining crude oil into the various usable oils ranging, at the top end, from aviation products and motor gasoline down to the lower end of fuel oils and diesel—which had been carried in ships of around nine to 12 thousand tonnes were moving up in size to ships of 18 to 20 thousand tonnes. These changes in ship size meant very substantial decreases in the cost of moving oil around the world and also meant a need for improvement in port facilities to accommodate the tankers throughout the world.

The oil industry is a very highly competitive business, and the marine part of the oil industry had its main competitive edge in ship size. If you could move your oil across the oceans of the world in ships substantially larger than your competitors', then that made a considerable difference. The rest of my time in Shell was largely related to the carriage of oil, gas and chemicals in ships larger, and therefore more economically efficient than those of the competition.

I, personally, found this very interesting, because it meant that one was in contact with all the other parts of the organisation for which one was working. I had dealings with both the production side of the business, where the oil was extracted from the ground and loaded into crude oil carrying tankers, and also the refining side of the business, where these tankers were discharged into the various refineries. The refined products then had to be carried to the various markets around the world, so one was also in contact with all one's marketing colleagues in the business.

These considerations ruled my life, effectively for all the rest of my time in Shell, finishing up, as I did, as the Director of the International Company, with the responsibility for Shell's movement of all its products over the seas of the world. There were two other areas which assumed ever larger proportions in my work; these were the questions of oil pollution and safety which I will enlarge upon later.

One of my first assignments was to travel out to Japan, to advise the local company there about their intent to build a refinery in Japan. Previously, Shell's products in Japan had been delivered in the refined state from refineries in other parts of the world, but there was a growing realisation all over the world that various countries should have refineries to refine their products in the places they were going to be distributed and used. The essential requirement in Japan was to find a site which would accommodate the increasingly large crude carrying tankers that were going to be used to take crude oil firstly from the Shell fields in Borneo and also from the Middle East to Japan. To this end I travelled quite extensively in Japan.

It was very interesting in those days. We lived in Japanese inns in the winter of 1954; they had a particularly cold November and December that year. I was struck by the fact that Japanese inns were not heated much at all; the only heat that one ever had was called a 'kibachi,' which was a huge jar filled with sand on which some hot coals were placed, and this gave out a very minimal amount of heat. Bearing in mind that the houses were built of wood and paper, it really did not make much impact on the temperature. It was customary in these little inns for the assembled company to take hot baths. All the inns I went to had these hot baths; some of them were fed by hot springs and others just used water boiled in the inn and put in the bath. The assembled company would all get into the bath together in the evening, and hope to heat themselves up enough to last them through the night.

As was usual, I was travelling with a Japanese company man, an engineer, and he was even more modest that I. I think everyone, when first confronted with the idea of getting into the bath with everyone in the evening, feels a bit embarrassed, but this chap decided that he would keep his kimono on, so when he got into the bath his kimono floated out and looked like a flower. All the people in the hotel came to watch this odd chap who insisted on keeping his kimono on in the bath!

I think that anyone going to Japan and having to conduct business there must find themselves in a very difficult situation. Apart from the difficulties of the Japanese language—of which I had no knowledge whatsoever—there is the cultural difference in terms of the way people think, the approach to problems, and so on, with which one has to become familiar.

I remember a fairly senior gentleman in the Shell organisation in Japan explaining to me that it would be quite unthinkable for a Japanese to go into a railway station, let us say in Tokyo, and say to an official in the station, 'When does the next train leave for Yokohama?' This is because such a question could place a man in extreme embarrassment, if he were expected to know, but didn't know the answer. So the technique would be to go to such a man and say, 'I am very interested in the possibility that I might be able to catch a train for Yokohama', and the man would therefore by able to answer, 'Well, indeed I may be able to help you in that matter, because I happen to know that the train leaves at (whatever time it might be).'

Also, whereas Europeans in a business discussion would be quite willing to say to one another that they didn't really believe that what a particular person was saying was so, and go on to produce a counter argument, this would have been quite difficult in Japan. I remember that in looking for this refinery site around several localities in Japan, our Japanese partner company decided they would produce a Japanese gentleman who would represent their interests in the marine aspects of the various sites that might be chosen for the refinery. For this purpose they chose a Japanese admiral, a charming old boy. Early on in our joint discussions at one of the possible locations, there was a matter which arose concerning the relationship between tidal height and tidal stream. With all my experience of Borneo and my hydrographic training in the Navy I thought I knew a fair bit about tides, and this Japanese admiral who was representing the marine interests of our partners expressed an opinion which I thought was just wrong. I was foolish enough to say so; when my interpreter translated what I had said there was a deathly hush and everyone went quite pale and I can remember thinking, 'What on earth have I done here?' My Shell colleague, from the local company with whom I was travelling, said, 'Now you've done it; it is apparent to me that you have said something which contradicts what this Japanese expert has said.' So I said indeed, I thought he was wrong. My Shell colleague told me that you just can't do that in Japan, and that it would take several days to sort out and so it proved. Apparently, in circumstances like this one would have to approach the matter very carefully and very delicately, and go all round the houses to eventually reach a position where the other expert might be able to accept your opinion without putting him in the wrong and causing him to lose face over the matter. Perhaps fortunately, it was decided that this site over which we had had this difficulty was not going to be suitable, for a whole lot of other reasons, and the matter didn't cause too serious a difficulty with our local Japanese partners.

Before leaving London for my assignment in Japan, I had been briefed by the people in the London office concerned with Eastern affairs that they would almost certainly want me to go over to Korea. Here they wanted me to make some assessments of the possibilities of supply of refined products to the United Nations forces, mainly Americans of course, in Korea, notably in the Ports of Inchon, Pusan and a small refinery at a place called Ulsan on the east coast of the Korean peninsula. I did indeed receive instructions to go to Korea, and I remember the Shell house in Seoul in Korea, which had been the residence of the manager with responsibility for Shell's affairs in Korea, was in an absolutely shocking condition. It had been occupied by the North Koreans when they had overrun Seoul in the early part of the Korean war; it was bare of any decent furniture and we slept on camp beds with only pretty awful grey blankets. It was, of course, very cold and we had virtually no heating; the food was not great either. My stay in Korea was not very pleasant. Travelling around was also extremely difficult. The local Shell chap and

I were given ranks; I was a temporary Lieutenant Colonel of the American Army, I remember. This was absolutely essential, because one couldn't get into any area of any military importance unless one had the necessary credentials.

In the event I made two visits to Korea from Japan. I remember on one occasion coming back in a four engined aircraft from Seoul to Tokyo, when we lost two of the engines on one side of the aircraft. It was a pretty horrible night, with a severe storm, and I can remember the Korean air hostess in the aircraft looking quite green. I suppose we all felt a bit green, because the aircraft was bucketing about all over the place. When we landed in Tokyo there were fire trucks and all sorts on the runway but the landing was perfectly successful and there was no damage done; still, it was one of the most frightening experiences I have ever had in the air.

Very fortunately for me, we managed to get the Japanese refinery site project all sorted out just before Christmas. This enabled me to go round the shops in Japan and buy some nice things for my wife and children. Japan was a very good shopping place for this purpose. One could buy lovely pearls for one's wife and the toys available were quite incredible. For relatively modest sums of money I was able to buy some lovely toys for all the children. I arrived home, having flown from Tokyo, I think on Christmas Eve. My wife was very pleased to see me, but she said to me, 'Well now you can get cracking and put up the Christmas decorations!' as she was pregnant—but I was absolutely exhausted and quite unable to help!

CHAPTER TWELVE

World Travel

I have already explained that the intent on the marine side of Shell was to improve the cost of delivery of petroleum anywhere in the world, by using the largest possible ships; this meant that many of the port facilities which the various Shell installations had around the world had to be made suitable for bigger tankers. In the office in London we kept an extensive record of all the facilities of all the tanker terminals around the world. Very commonly our colleagues, on the production side of the business, the manufacturing, or refining, side of the business, and in the marketing areas where the refined oil was delivered were in touch with the authorities to try to improve the port facilities to take bigger and bigger tankers as the years went on. So in the Marine Office in London we were constantly updating our port facilities records of the tanker berths in all the world ports, and not only Shell ports, because very often by exchange arrangements with other oil companies we would be delivering cargoes to facilities which were not owned by Shell companies. It was a very complicated business in the international oil business, because it was very common to buy and sell cargoes between the various competing oil companies.

As I have already said, this was very interesting because it brought one in contact with one's Shell colleagues right across the spectrum of the international business. At this time Shell was very anxious to regionalise its activities. For instance, when I first went to Japan, nearly all the Shell installations in Japan were headed up by either British or Dutch personnel from the holding companies back in the UK and Holland; this was the case around most of the world. However, there was a drive to change this, and to employ people from each country in all aspects of the business in the various companies. For instance, in the producing companies in the Arab world, there was a desire to try to bring up and train local people to take on responsibilities and to move further up the ladder of responsibility at local level. Exactly the same thing happened in the refining companies, and there was a drive to use local people. This was really very interesting, because it meant that one met people of all nationalities in the various parts of the world where one had to go, and of course my travelling commitments at this time were enormously extensive.

I spent quite a lot of time back in the Caribbean. The islands to the north were supplied from the refinery in Curacao with refined petroleum products, but the marketing companies in these various islands were run by the Shell Company of the West Indies which was based in Kingston, Jamaica. So on many occasions I visited Haiti, The Dominican Republic—which is the country on the other side of the island of Hispaniola to Haiti—and also San Juan, Puerto Rico. In all these countries the problem was to try to find facilities and depots which would accommodate the large product carriers of 18 to 20 thousand tonnes dead weight.

The island of Cuba was also supplied from Curacao, but in accordance with the general idea of having refineries built in the various countries of utilisation of the refined petroleum products, there was a plan to have a refinery in Cuba. I was asked to report on this, and I came to the conclusion that by far the best marine possibility was the Port of Havana, which fortunately suited the marketing arrangements for the products to be manufactured in the refinery. So, I was able to recommend dredging of a channel to get the large crude carrying tankers, around 35 thousand tonnes dead weight, in to the jetty at Havana. As was common at that time, I was associated with an engineer who happened to be from the Dutch side of the Shell organisation; it was his responsibility to determine how the berth for the tanker should be built. I was responsible for assessing what was necessary in the way of width of channel, dredging possibilities and the turning area and tug facilities which would be necessary to handle these big ships. Cuba, at that time, was a dictatorship under the sway of Batista. In accordance with Shell's regionalisation policy the chief executive of the local Shell Company was a Cuban, one Julio Iglesias, who was a very interesting and colourful character. I remember he drove a bright red Buick convertible of which he was very proud, it had all the modern trimmings for the time: white sidewall tyres and bright chromium everywhere. It was his pride and joy.

In addition to the problems I had in respect of the supply of crude to the refinery, I also had to consider the problems involved in the supply of products from the Havana refinery to the various ports in the island of Cuba by product carrying tankers of around 18 to 20 thousand tonnes dead weight. The chap in charge of operations and engineering in the Cuban Company at that time was a chap called Paddy Riley, who became a very close friend of mine. He was a most interesting and amusing chap. He was also a very keen driver of fast and powerful cars. He had an

Oldsmobile, with a four barrel carburettor, which he used to drive round the roads of Cuba at around 100 miles an hour!

At that time Cuba was very close to the United States in terms of the two main products from the island, which were fruit and sugar. It was quite interesting going around the various ports on the island of Cuba: any mention of the fact that we were associated with Julio Iglesias, who was a friend of Batista, immediately meant that all the officials would spring to attention and treat us with great respect. Even at that time I was aware of the fact that there was a very strong anti-American feeling in that country.

About this time in my Shell career, the company had an executive course for young people, I suppose in their mid-thirties, who were in some degree of managerial positions in the company. I was sent on this course, and I found it extremely interesting. The first part of it was in Shell Lodge, near Teddington; a big house owned by Shell. It was quite fascinating; we were lectured to by senior people from the London office on all aspects of the business and the assembled company of people on the course were very international. There was one from Venezuela, one from Brazil, several Dutchmen of course, a number of Frenchmen and one or two people from the Middle East. Broadly speaking, at that time the British side of Shell was concerned with the marketing of products around the world, the finance of the company and the marine, and it was these aspects of the business which were studied during our time in Shell Lodge. We then went over to the Hague. The Dutch side of Shell at that time was primarily concerned with the exploration and production of oil, and the manufacturing and technical side of the then developing large scale chemical business; it was these aspects that we studied in our time in Holland. The course finally divided into two parts: one went to Germany and the other to France. The purpose of this was to study integrated business of a really large Shell company, the one operating in Germany and the one operating in France. I was fortunate enough to go to the French side of the business, which again I found most interesting.

On completion of the Shell Lodge course, I resumed my travelling round the various companies operating in the world. I remember going to the east coast of Africa visiting Kenya and Tanganyika and also the islands of Madagascar and Reunion, all of which was time consuming, and not very pleasant once again for my long-suffering wife. I was away for quite long periods and she had to manage with five children. It seemed to be almost predictable that when I was going away on a long trip, just before I left or immediately after, one of the children would be ill, and she had to deal with all the problems that a parent had to without the support of a husband.

My next assignment involved a visit to the United States of America, because the American Shell Company, Shell Oil, were at that time becoming interested in offshore drilling, particularly in the Gulf of Mexico. The Dutch side of the business, which, as I have said, had responsibility for the technical aspects of exploration and production, felt it would be useful to have someone from the marine side of the business to go over to America to look at the problems of supply of equipment to offshore oil exploration and production activities. A team of two, a naval architect and myself, were sent over to liaise with the American company to make some recommendations about the supply of materials to offshore drilling rigs. We eventually came to the conclusion that the craft that should be built and used for this sort of work would involve fairly powerful vessels—twin screw with a very clear afterdeck for all sorts of material, drill pipe, drilling mud materials and all the stores that were necessary to conduct offshore operations. The control part of the ship would be at the fore-end and the ship would be left with an open afterdeck. It could then be manoeuvred out to the rig and place its anchors well out and back up to the rig, put lines onto the rig, and then the materials could be lifted onto the drilling rig with suitable cranes. Perhaps not surprisingly, we found that all the other companies operating in the Gulf Of Mexico had come to exactly similar conclusions and a lot of craft of this type had already been built.

My next assignment was a trip to the Arabian Gulf; the prime purpose of my visit was to advise on the building of a tanker terminal to load crude oil from the fields in Iran. Previously, all the oilfields in Iran had been operated by BP, but after the nationalisation of oil by the government at the time, BP no longer had responsibility for the production of oil. A consortium of companies was formed to produce and export oil from the very large Iranian oilfields which were then being discovered. In addition to Shell and BP, all the major American oil companies had some share in the business so there were marine representatives of all the various companies involved in the investigations. It had been established that the probable site for a large tanker terminal to take the big crude oil carriers should be at Kharg Island off the west coast of Iran. However, when this multi-national company of marine people arrived on site, we found that the civil engineers had designed a berth which lay across the tidal streams and we came to the conclusion that this was probably a very unwise thing to do. So we recommended that the plans should be completely changed and that the jetties should be built so as to line up with the tidal currents in that part of the Arabian Gulf. This didn't please the civil engineering consultants, who had been retained by the company to advise on the building of the jetties, because the proposals which we made were going to be more expensive. The result of all this was that there was a major meeting called in Tehran, where a confrontation occurred between the civil engineering advisors and the marine representatives of the various companies. At the end of the day the marine people won out, because the senior management of the consortium of oil companies were afraid to build terminals where the marine advisors said there would be serious problems, and possibly accidents both to the structure and to the ships coming alongside.

At the same time I visited Kuwait, where Shell had concluded a deal to buy the proportion of the Kuwait Oil Company's crude oil which was owned by the Gulf Oil Company, an American company operating jointly with BP to produce oil from Kuwait fields.

I then went down to Qatar and joined my boss, one John Kirby, who was in charge of all Shell's marine operations at that time. My boss and I were invited to dinner at the house of the general manager of the Qatar Company. We duly arrived at the general manager's house where there was obviously some confusion, because an invitation had arrived from the Sheikh of Qatar inviting the chief executive of the Marine part of the Shell Company and myself to dinner. 'Mrs Shell General Manager' made it quite clear that we could go to the Sheikh's dinner party, but that we had to be back for her dinner party at a later time. This seemed to me to be a very awkward turn of events, because not only were we going to have to eat two dinners but I couldn't see how we were going to fit everything in.

However, when we arrived at the Sheikh's palace it was really quite extraordinary. The Sheikh obviously didn't use alcohol and there were no preliminaries. We were invited into a beautiful room in his palace with the most gorgeous carpets, and there in the centre of this vast room was a round table with chairs all around it. The Sheikh and his people sat on the one side and the Shell General Manager of the local company and my boss and I sat on the other side of this table. In no time a huge dish was brought in with saffron rice and on top of the dish was a dead sheep, beautifully cooked but in its entirety! As soon as this big dish was put down in the centre of the table, everybody made a grab for what they thought was the best bit of the sheep. Whilst all the trappings of the palace were absolutely magnificent, I thought it quite strange and incongruous that the plates on which we were going to eat this

116

sheep—with our fingers of course—were the sort of plates that I had been used to at boy scout camps: a white enamel with a blue border. During the entire meal nobody said anything. I suppose it would have been fairly difficult to carry on a conversation, because although the Sheikh himself had a reasonable understanding of English, most of his other Arab guests had no English at all. They were desert Sheikhs and very tough looking chaps. Not only that, but all the attendants standing around the table had sub-machine guns hanging from their shoulders and huge daggers at their waists. I am sure the dinner lasted no more than a quarter of an hour—that was all it took to dispose of the sheep. An interesting thing was that during the meal the table was very brightly lit, but I was conscious of a number of people lurking in the gloom away from the table. I thought they must be some more of the sub-machine gun slaves. In the Gulf Sheikhdoms most of the Sheikh's attendants were slaves. However, when the Sheikh and his guests had finished their attack on the sheep, he raised his hand, and all these fellows came rushing out of the gloom with two gallon buckets and scooped up as much of the mutton and rice as they could get hold of. The next course was fruit, which was limited to oranges and that took, I suppose, another five minutes. Then all the guests, the Arabs and the Europeans, were lined up, and a chap came along with an enormous coffee jug with a very elegant spout and we all had tiny little cups. This chap, with great dexterity, fired coffee into each little cup as he passed down the line. I had been advised that the drill was that if you wanted some more coffee, you drank your coffee and held your cup out, and the chap came rattling down the line again with his huge coffee pot; if you didn't want any more coffee then you would waggle your cup slightly and he would pass by. I found the coffee most unappetising; it was very heavily flavoured with cardamom and very bitter, so I was happy to waggle my cup. The result of this was that we were able to get back to 'Mrs General Manager's' dinner party in fairly good order, having eaten not too much and in adequate time to have our drinks before her dinner.

When we sat down to dinner, I found myself sitting next to a chap who had been introduced as Mohammed Mardi but I knew from the way he spoke that he was a Scotsman, so I asked him which part of Scotland he came from. He said that he was sure that I would never have heard of it so I said, 'Well try me.' He said, 'It's a village in Angus called Bowriefauld.' Well my mother had been left a house in Bowriefauld and I knew it well. So I asked him what his name had been before it became Mohammed Mardi, and he said it was Cochran, so I said that I knew his brother very well indeed. It so happened that a chap working a small farm when I used to visit this house in Bowriefauld as a boy, was a chap called Will Cochran and he indeed was the brother of Mohammed Mardi who had gone out to Qatar as a young man. He was a very soldierly sort of chap and had impressed the Sheikh as to his military abilities, so that he had eventually been promoted to head up the Sheikh's police force, which was in fact an army. I thought it was very interesting. It seemed to me at that time that the various Sheikhdoms around the Gulf were very much like the Scottish clan system. The situation was that each Sheikh was very nervous of the territorial ambitions of his next door neighbour, but was quite prepared to be friendly with Sheikhdoms further away from his own particular territory. Another similarity was that the clan chiefs in Scotland had normally ascended to their position by heredity, but that depended on general agreement amongst the clan that the man succeeding to the position of chief was sufficiently warlike and generally competent to do a good job. If he was not, then steps had to be taken, and usually the poor chap was disposed of by some convenient means. Exactly the same situation seemed to apply to the Sheikhdoms around the Gulf.

At that time, the oil produced from the Qatar fields was loaded into tankers lying at buoy moorings off the coast, but the Company were already exploring in the sea off the coast of Qatar. I knew that my colleagues in the Hague were beginning to concern themselves with how the oil from the offshore fields was going to be brought back to the shore and loaded into tankers at these buoy moorings. I had come to the conclusion that it might be possible to berth a tanker offshore in the vicinity of the offshore fields, at a single buoy mooring, and then bring loading tankers alongside this effective depot ship so they could then be loaded from the depot ship. To investigate this further, we chartered a small dhow to take us out to have a look around the offshore fields. The fellows manning the dhow were pretty evil-looking chaps and I remember being slightly concerned, because at that time my wife had very kindly given me a beautiful gold Longines wrist watch with a gold bracelet and these chaps were looking quite longingly at my watch. However, I needn't have worried—in my experience these Arab chaps were very honest and they certainly wouldn't have thought of stealing your watch.

From Qatar I went down to Oman, where another Shell company was already producing small quantities of oil but hoping to produce much larger quantities from fields there. Muscat, the capital of Oman, is an absolutely fascinating Arab town. The town itself is built around the old harbour of Muscat, which is a dhow harbour, and it was a walled town with a huge gate which even in those days was closed at night, with nobody being allowed in or out. As far as I could make out, no Omani regarded himself as being properly dressed if he didn't carry a 303 Lee Enfield service rifle with a bandoleer of beautifully polished brass cartridges around his shoulder.

At that time in the marine office in London big changes were afoot. Whereas previously all the marine operations had been handled by a company, Shell Tankers Ltd, it was decided that Shell Tankers would become a company with sole responsibility for the owning and operation of the British tanker fleet. Another company, Shell International Marine, was to be set up to look after all aspects of the Shell group's marine activities and to charter ships from the various Shell Tanker owning companies, notably in Britain and Holland. This meant a great change in the whole organisation of the marine part of Shell in the London office.

My nautical superior at this time, Captain Golds, retired, and I was promoted to the position of Chief Marine Superintendent of Shell International Marine, and effectively the nautical advisor to the Shell Group of companies. This obviously increased my areas of responsibility very substantially, and I think my wife hoped that it would reduce my travelling commitments. However, as the years went on, we found that this was not to be, and I still travelled the world extensively. However, most of the trips I made were of shorter duration than they had been in previous years.

At this time I had been conscious of the fact that, with the ever increasing size of crude oil tankers required to move crude oil mainly from the Middle East to Europe, the problems involved in mooring the tankers were becoming more and more difficult to solve. In some major oil loading ports like Kuwait, where there was reasonably deep water fairly close to the shore, it was possible to build tanker berths at a reasonable cost to accommodate these very big ships. However, where deep water was a considerably longer distance offshore the cost of providing normal jetty facilities alongside for tankers was prohibitive, and it was common to use buoy moorings. The difficulty was that as these ships became bigger, the difficulty of obtaining a buoy berth involved very serious problems. Another consideration was that manoeuvring a very big ship into a fixed buoy mooring presented quite serious difficulties in bad weather, and quite substantial delays could be experienced. It was obvious to me that the mooring forces could be very much reduced, and the difficulties of getting a ship onto a buoy could be substantially eased, if the ship could be put to a single buoy around which she could swing and be aligned to whatever might be the prevailing forces at any given time. My naval experience had also taught me that it was a very easy matter to take a ship to a single buoy—a much more simple manoeuvre than trying to manoeuvre a ship into a complicated number of buoys with the ship held in the fixed position.

I enlisted the help of my good friend, Joop Langeveldt, who had been in charge of the civil engineering aspects of the offshore drilling activities in Trinidad, and had by this time reached the position of being the Chief Civil Engineer of the Dutch side of the company in the Hague. Together we undertook a series of investigations in a hydraulic laboratory in Wageningen in Holland. Model experimentation in this laboratory led us to believe that we were on an absolute winner, and that we could provide buoy moorings which would be operable in far worse weather conditions than the existing multi-buoy arrangements, and also that it would be very much easier for tankers to approach and moor to and that berthing times could be very much reduced. The problem then was to find somewhere in the world where we could put down the first single buoy mooring.

It was fortunate that the company operating in Borneo, my old stamping ground, were thinking of extending their buoy moorings to take larger ships. They, and we, were readily convinced that it would be sensible to try this novel arrangement for an offshore loading facility for tankers. We designed and laid the first single buoy mooring in the world in Borneo. In order to allow the ship to swing freely around the buoy through 360 degrees, there had to be an oil-tight swivel in the buoy; from the buoy a floating hose had to be taken to the mid-ships of the ship where the loading terminal of the tanker was situated. We were advised by the hose manufacturers that they could design a hose that would float in the water when full of oil; however, when we got the equipment out to Borneo and on site the first thing that happened was that when the hose was filled with oil it wasn't sufficiently buoyant and it sank.

However, any difficulties attached to the operation of the single buoy mooring in Borneo proved to be teething troubles, and the operating company were highly satisfied with the results. The buoy mooring was seen to be more readily accessible, the time taken to moor the ship up and have her loading was reduced substantially, and it was generally felt that in areas where weather conditions might be more severe than Borneo, moorings of this type would have a great advantage.

CHAPTER THIRTEEN

Widening Responsibilities

The success of the single buoy mooring in Borneo led to very extensive discussions inside Shell. It had to be decided what attitude we should take to, on the one hand, the need to keep a technique inside the company where it could be of substantial advantage to the company, and on the other hand, the need to ensure that where we had facilities shared jointly with other companies, the advantages of the single buoy mooring could be and should be adequately deployed.

It was immediately apparent that the single buoy mooring would only really be suitable for operations involving one grade of oil; this virtually meant that it would be restricted to loading and discharge facilities for crude oil, that is crude oil to be loaded from the various producing areas of the world and discharged into facilities supplying crude oil to the various refineries. It was decided, after extensive discussion inside the Shell group of companies, that the best interest of the Shell group would be in sharing our knowledge and our expertise very freely throughout the rest of the industry.

It immediately became apparent that, whilst the American oil companies were very ready to accept the proposition that it would be sensible to have a body to ensure a degree of standardisation around the industry—so that ships of any particular part of the industry could go to buoy moorings owned by any other part and find there was a common usage of mooring arrangements and hose connections—they also indicated the most severe concern about the anti-trust considerations that might relate to this.

The American companies, in effect, made it very clear that whilst they would be very happy to co-operate in any group, they would require that the group should be attended in all its meetings by expert anti-trust lawyers from the various companies. It was further agreed that the proceedings of any meetings which might take place would be recorded and promulgated extensively throughout the industry. So a body to be called the 'Single Point Mooring Forum' was set up, and I was asked to be its chairman. The reason it was called the 'Single Point Mooring Forum' and not the 'Single Buoy Mooring Forum' was because, at that time, there were those in the industry who thought that it might prove to be more advantageous to use pillars rather than buoys to moor the tankers.

There were in the Shell group of companies two pressing problems to which the single buoy mooring might provide an answer. One was the supply of crude oil to a company run by Shell's partner in Japan, in Niigata, where the cost of the development of the Port of Niigata to take the very large crude carriers necessary to carry the crude economically from the Middle East to Japan would be completely prohibitive. So, I travelled to Japan with an engineer from the Dutch side of the Shell organisation, the purpose of the visit being to convince our partners, Showa Oil Company, who operated the refinery, that the single buoy mooring which could be laid off the Port of Niigata connected by pipeline to the refinery would provide an economical answer to their problems. After lengthy discussions in Japan, it was agreed that the single buoy mooring could be a very suitable solution to the problem in the summer. However, Japanese colleagues were very afraid of the winter conditions in the Sea of Japan, so it was agreed that, at the start up of single buoy mooring operations, the buoy would only be operated in the summer, and they would restrict the port to ships of a size that could enter the harbour during the winter months.

A similar problem existed in Durban, and on my way back from Japan I went to South Africa where there were two problems. The first was to convince the South Africa government that a single buoy mooring would be an acceptable way of discharging crude oil through a pipeline to the refineries in Durban. In addition to the Shell refinery, there was another refinery run by an American company. In the event, we were successful in both of these objectives. The South African authorities agreed to the placing of a single buoy mooring off the coast of Natal, which would feed both the Shell and Standard Vacuum refineries in South Africa, and the American oil company involved in the other refinery also agreed that this would be a good way of providing access of crude to their refinery.

A 'Single Point Mooring Forum' meeting had been arranged in New York, to take place immediately after the South African meeting. This meant that I had to travel through London directly to New York. My long-suffering wife was prepared to come and meet me at the airport; all I had time to do was to change aircraft on arriving from South Africa to catch a plane to New York. She was kind enough to bring me a change of clothing; we only had time to have a quick kiss, and I was off again.

The first meeting of the 'Single Point Mooring Forum' in New York was really quite successful. There was considerable enthusiasm around the industry for the Forum; it was quite obvious that the other companies were very interested in developing discharge terminals and, for that matter, loading terminals, using the single buoy moorings. I recall that on completion of the discussions in New York I caught the night flight back to London. In those days it was quite common for all of my colleagues in the oil industry to be prepared to fly overnight from New York to London and then be in the office the following day. This wasn't because we were under any pressure, but we were all doing very interesting jobs at that time, and we were very anxious to get back to our offices and deal with problems that had arisen during our absence. So, as was customary, I went home and had a change of clothing and went straight into the office—and I found that I was suffering from quite a severe disturbance in my balance. I went to the Shell medicos and they could find nothing wrong. My wife said, 'Well, you've been travelling far too much and you are just exhausted.' I think she may well have been right. The company were kind enough to provide me with a car to go to the office every day, which relieved me of the worries of catching trains with the disturbance in my balance, and in a few days I was right back to normal.

Certainly, travelling around the world for Shell in those days was as pleasant as the company could possibly make it. One always travelled first class in aircraft, which made a great deal of difference to the fatigue one suffered through long distance travelling. On arrival in any part of the world one expected to be met by a representative of the local Shell company with an envelope containing money, and the company had arrangements whereby one was paid a daily allowance which covered one's hotel expenses and so on. This greatly eased the problem of accounting for expenses. These considerations certainly reduced the amount of fatigue that many of us who were travelling extensively around the world at that time suffered.

In the Shell group of companies the employment of single buoy moorings went ahead at a considerable pace: a mooring was put into place in Port Dickson to supply the Shell refining operation in Malaysia, and single buoy moorings were also laid in Oman and Qatar to export crude from these two countries.

As I have said, we had decided in principle to extend our knowledge in any way we possibly could to joint companies in which Shell had an interest. To that end, I made a trip around a number of the loading installations in the Middle East. Shell had concluded a deal with Occidental Petroleum Company to buy a proportion of their production from the Libyan oilfield with tanker loading terminals in the Gulf of Sidra in Libya, I went to Libya and there met the marine people in charge of the operation. I found them generally receptive, and I was able to take the marine superintendent of the loading operation to Qatar, where we were able to demonstrate to him what we thought to be the advantages of single buoy mooring loading terminals.

Shell, at that time, also had an interest in the Iraq petroleum company, which was exporting its oil from the Iraqi fields through the loading terminals in the Eastern Mediterranean, the oil being taken from the Iraqi fields by pipeline to the loading terminals. I remember driving over from Damascus to Beirut, and thinking what a beautiful country the Lebanon was in those days, and Beirut was a very sophisticated and very pleasant city. This, of course, was long before the severe troubles that the country of Lebanon suffered with Israel.

It was quite obvious, of course, that single buoy moorings were not the answer to all the problems involved in the loading and discharge facilities for crude oil. Wherever sheltered water could be found, jetties alongside which the ships could lie were provided. The loading arrangements at Kharg Island, and those at Kuwait, were typical examples.

Similarly, at the discharge end of the voyage, the ideal arrangement was the provision of sheltered harbours, in which suitable alongside discharge berths could be provided. This was particularly true of North-west Europe. The largest developing port in north-west Europe for the discharge of crude oil was Rotterdam, where the wise old Dutch city fathers of Rotterdam had decided to extend their port seaward and to cater for, they hoped, as much of the trade into the whole of Europe as they could possibly handle. However, the dredging costs involved in providing an adequate channel into deep water in the North Sea from the Port of Rotterdam were going to be quite enormous. A lot of attention was paid to the width and depth of channel which would be necessary, and also to the optimum direction to reduce the dredging as far as could be possible done.

Shell derived considerable benefit from the fact that one of its parents, of course, was a Dutch company. I had some very interesting discussions with the maritime and civil engineering authorities in Holland about the problems involved in providing adequate channel access to the port of Rotterdam. I remember one of the things we did was to buoy the potential channel and see whether the pilots could conduct the ships with adequate safety in the given channel widths by reducing the buoys until the appropriate measurement was achieved. Another important factor, of course, was what depth was necessary; this led to a great deal of concern about the matter of underkeel clearance—that is, the amount of water that has to be allowed beneath the draught of the incoming ship to ensure adequate safety. It was well known, and had been well known for many years, that any ship underway squats in the water, that is it goes deeper underway than it does in an absolutely motionless condition in the water. It was, however, quite unknown just how much the draught of the ship would be affected by its speed through the water.

A waterway of enormous interest to the oil industry at this time was the Suez Canal, because following the clearing of the canal of block ships which had been laid after the war with Egypt, tankers were again beginning to use the canal on the voyage from the Arabian Gulf loading terminals to North-west Europe. So, in Shell it was decided that we would undertake some investigations with one of the laboratories, and the French laboratory in Grenoble was chosen. Extensive work was put in hand to do two things—to investigate the effect of underkeel clearance on ships going through waterways, and also to study the whole question of underkeel clearance known as squat, which ships would suffer underway in any given circumstances.

The laboratory in Grenoble did some wonderful work, and they did come up with a formula by which one could calculate the effect on underkeel clearance of ships navigating narrow channels. They also did some very interesting work on the return current, that is the flow of water past a ship forcing her way through a narrow channel. This was of great interest to the civil engineers concerned with channel maintenance, because it is the speed of that current which causes considerable erosion of the banks of a waterway.

It was decided that my then boss, one John Kirby, and I should pay a visit to the Suez Canal, and there we met the man who was in charge of the canal, one Mohammed Younis. This was, of course, a relatively short time after the Anglo-French action against Egypt, and we expected that we would get a fairly frosty and almost hostile reception from Mohammed Younis and his staff. This did not prove to be the case—he was a very pleasant man, and we got on very well with him. He made it quite clear that he would welcome what we could do to help him in his decisions concerning what were the largest tankers he could put through his existing canal, and equally importantly, how the canal could be most economically developed for even larger ships. He also wanted our help on the matters of what channel width and depth were necessary for any given ship size, and what sort of difficulties would be expected in maintenance of the banks. During our discussions with Younis it became apparent that we shared quite an interest in fishing. He said that he would like to take us on a fishing trip, which he did. He took us to Port Said and it was really the strangest fishing trip—I have fished in many parts of the world, in all sorts of different conditions, for all sorts of fish, but this was perhaps one of the most interesting trips. On a suitable quay in the harbour of Port Said there were basket chairs arranged, each basket chair had a table beside it with adequate supplies of soft drinks. Being a Muslim country of course there was no alcohol. We were invited to sit in these chairs, and we had huge long bamboo rods on which fellows standing behind us put bait. All we had to do was to cast the rod forwards so that the bait went into the water, where it was very soon snapped up by a mullet. All one then had to do was to jerk the rod quickly back over one's head and the mullet flew over to a chap who was ready to take it off the hook and re-bait the hook. Fishing, you might say, made very easy!

These discussions in Egypt resulted in Younis being invited to London. We had a meeting conducted by the Shell Managing Director with marine responsibilities, at which it was agreed that I would be sent out again to Egypt. The Suez Canal Company were kind enough to accommodate me in their magnificent canal buildings in Ismailia. The accommodation was quite palatial, but I had no company. I was very glad every now and then to make a trip to Cairo and spend a little time with my Shell colleagues there.

The Suez Canal Authority had employed a number of professors from the two universities in Cairo—the Cairo University and Ainshams University. These were charming gentlemen but they were a little bit too academic for my liking and I found great difficulty in getting any real ideas as to how the work might be taken forward. This changed when the Suez Canal appointed a young engineer called Nabil Hilay, whom I found a very practical and switched on chap. In no time at all we had agreed that what should be done was that I would go back to London and consult with the various instrument makers who made echo-sounding gear. This equipment is used to detect the amount of water underneath ships; we needed it modified so that it could be put on the bottom of the Suez Canal. Instead of shining downwards from the bottom of the ship with a sound beam, it would shine upwards from the bottom of the canal. It would measure, as ships went past, what the underkeel clearance was over the whole length of the ship, and would therefore measure squat. We could also measure the return current with suitable current meters.

In the meantime, Mohammed Younis had fallen foul of President Nasser. As far as I can understand, his brother, who was very anti-Nasser, had plotted to blow up the President. The result of this was that the whole family was in absolute disgrace, and Mohammed Younis disappeared from the scene. I believe he went to Lebanon, but we never had any further contact with him. He was, however, succeeded by another equally friendly and charming man called Mashur Achmed Mashur.

On return to London I was able to get the instrument makers to make suitable echo-sounding equipment to put on the bottom of the canal, along with current-measuring devices to measure the return current as the ship went through the canal. When all the instrumentation was complete I returned to Egypt to conduct the full scale investigations. I found Mashur just as pleasant as his predecessor; he was kind enough to put his personal car at my disposal, which meant that I didn't have to spend all my time in Ismailiya. I could pay visits to Cairo, where of course I had become friendly with the Shell staff. Cairo, at that time, was a very attractive city.

The engineer in chief of Shell on the marketing side of the business at that time was in contact with an international organisation, the Permanent International Association of Navigation Congresses. The word 'Navigation' in the acronym PIANC really didn't refer to the art of navigation, but rather navigation in the sense of canals and waterways. It was, in fact, an international body comprising engineers from the various ports around the world. My engineering colleague introduced me to this body and I felt that, bearing in mind our problems relating to development of port facilities for very large ships, this would be an ideal body with which to have an association. I therefore sought election to the British committee of PIANC, and I was able to persuade the international organisation that it would be desirable for them to set up an international body, the purpose of which would be to concern itself with the development of port facilities for very big ships. The association holds congresses every four years in various parts of the world; I was able to take my wife to congresses in Scandinavia, France and in this country.

PIANC is a distinguished body; the conferences were always very well organised and attended by top people in the various countries in which they were held. I certainly found the technical discussions very useful. Harbour authorities tended to be very nervous about the large tankers being brought in to trade, and I found the technical discussions and the journals of PIANC a very good way of demonstrating the technicalities of matters such as channel width and depth required for any given size of tanker. These were matters of huge financial consequence to harbour authorities, so they were taking a very close interest in the development of knowledge in this area.

Another matter with very significant cost implications was the tug provision necessary to handle very large tankers. I came to the conclusion early on that the tug size and power should increase in rough proportion to the increase in the size of ships to be handled. In fact, I believed that it should be possible to handle any size of ship with only two tugs in all reasonable circumstances. It only required the tugs to be of adequate power, and that it would be possible to make the towing connection between the tug and the ship sufficiently strong, because breaking of tow ropes could be very bad news when a ship was being manoeuvred in close waters.

These ideas did not immediately appeal to the companies around north-west Europe whose business it was to supply adequate tugs to handle ships in the various ports. However, one of our major ports was Tranmere in the River Mersey, where crude carrying tankers feeding the refinery in Stanlow were berthed. I was able to convince the towage company there at the time that it would be in their best interests, and in ours, for them to build new powerful tugs so that they could handle ships with only two tugs where previously they had used four. The towage company agreed to build these powerful tugs, and my wife and I were invited to the launch of the first one in a yard in Devon called Appledore. It was a very pleasant occasion; the launching party were accommodated in the house which belonged to Christie, the man who had built the Glyndebourne Opera House in Surrey. The party arrived in the afternoon; the launch was to be in the afternoon of the following day. The Rolls Royce which belonged to this house was made available to the launch guests, and it was very enjoyable to drive around the Devon countryside. I remember the weather being very pleasant. The launch of any ship is always a nerve-racking occasion for the shipyard building the ship, because things can go wrong—and in this particular case, things did go wrong. The yard was by far the most important source of employment in the small town of Appledore, so the entire town had turned out to see the launch of this tug. When the vessel was halfway down the launching ways, the heavy timbers supporting the vessel gave way. The ship tilted over to an angle of about 45 degrees and huge balks of timber went flying up like matchsticks. It was most fortunate that none of these heavy balks of timber landed in the area where people were standing watching the launch of the vessel.

A second tug of similar size and power was launched, and the experience with these two tugs demonstrated quite clearly that it was perfectly possible and, in fact, economically very desirable, to handle these huge tankers with only two tugs, providing they had sufficient power. The promulgation of the experience in the Mersey made it possible to convince other cargo-operating companies in the other ports of north-west Europe that this was the way most economically to provide tug assistance with very big ships.

The Mersey was a very important waterway as far as Shell was concerned, because originally our refinery at Stanlow had been supplied by ships going up the Manchester Ship Canal. Then, when the first supertankers of around 30 thousand tonnes came into service, a new dock was built at Eastham, at the entrance to the Manchester Ship Canal. The oil was then sent by pipeline to Stanlow. The new dock at Eastham proved to be very disappointing for two reasons. Firstly, the dock itself was only big enough for the ships of 30 thousand tonnes, which were very quickly replaced by far larger crude carriers bringing crude oil into north-west Europe. Secondly, the part of the Mersey immediately seaward of the Eastham dock began to silt up seriously. My old mentor Doctor Ringers, who was then still a consultant to the Shell group of companies, was asked to investigate what could be done to improve the maintenance of depth in this channel leading into the dock. A considerable amount of dredging effort was being deployed to try to improve the depth in this difficult area. Doctor Ringers asked me to calculate the amount of spoil being removed, and the amount of siltation which was occurring. He then asked me to accompany him to the Mersey, where he made some further calculations about the totality of the dredging effort in the River Mersey and the bar outside the inner harbours. Doctor Ringers then concluded that the total amount of dredging effort which had been deployed over many years in the Mersey was greater than the volume of the tidal compartment—that is, it would have been just as efficient to start dredging with no original estuary at all! This led him to a decision in principle that it was really inefficient to carry on doing what had been for so long. For years, dredge materials from the inner channels had been taken out and dumped at sea; he came to the conclusion that the only way the matter could be improved was to keep the dredging spoil onshore. He therefore required me to go around the environs in close proximity to the Mersey, to find somewhere where he could dump huge quantities of dredging spoil. I felt it my duty to advise him that whilst this might be a solution which would readily be acceptable in Holland, it was extremely unlikely to be popular here, since he was proposing to dump huge quantities of dredging spoil which would have to pass through highly developed areas. I did, however, do what I was told to do, and I found large areas in the vicinity of Frodsham where certainly huge quantities of dredging spoil could be deposited. However, discussions that we had with the harbour authorities concerned—that is, the Mersey Docks and Harbour Board as it was in those days, and the

Manchester Ship Canal Company—immediately reinforced my view that the possibility of getting planning permission to have huge pipes running through the highly developed area of Cheshire just wasn't a feasible proposition, and Doctor Ringers had to abandon his ideas. It was then decided to build a model in the hydraulic laboratory in Wallingford, which was done. I fear that although the work done with the Wallingford model gave some quite interesting information about the Mersey, it didn't really go any great way to solving the dredging problems. However, as far as I was concerned, it was quite interesting, because I was invited to join the Board of the laboratory and I sat on that board until my retirement from Shell some years later.

CHAPTER FOURTEEN

Maritime Safety Matters

A t this time I had a seat on the General Council of the Chamber of Shipping, which was the body in the United Kingdom which looked after shipping affairs generally. I had been worried for some time about reports from our Masters relating to their concern about the risk of collision due to the heavy traffic in the Dover Straits. I voiced my concern about these matters in the various committees in the Chamber of Shipping dealing with maritime safety, and suggested that some thought should be given to the desirability of a routing arrangement in the Channel to keep the traffic into and out of the North Sea separate. To opinions along these lines, I got a very frosty reception indeed from my confreres in the Chamber of Shipping. However, a Frenchman called Commandant Oudet, who was a very active member in the Institute of Navigation, started to promulgate very similar ideas in the Institute. I had a seat on the Council of the Institute and I found the General Secretary, one Michael Ritchie, very enthusiastic to follow up the ideas which Oudet and I were advancing. Michael Ritchie sounded out his opposite numbers in the Navigational Institutes in France, Holland and Germany, and found somewhat to his surprise that they had been thinking along similar lines. As a result of all this, a meeting was arranged in Brighton under the auspices of the International Consultative body of the navigation institutes of the various European countries. There were virtually no dissenting voices at the meeting in Brighton, and it was agreed that an international group would be set up to prescribe voluntary routing arrangements for the Straits of Dover.

I think we were fortunate in that the media, in the shape of television, radio and the press, had taken a close interest in the proceedings in Brighton. We were supported very strongly by the media to press ahead with these arrangements. I had had close contact with the hydrographic department of the Royal Navy over many years, and I was asked by the Institute of Navigation to ask the hydrographer, Admiral Richie, whether he could promulgate the proposed traffic routing arrangements which this committee would outline in his notices to mariners. Steve Ritchie, quite understandably, said that he didn't think he could do that, because the matter would be on a purely voluntary basis and he didn't think that he could lend full naval authority to provisions which were not in any way mandatory. Another problem was that Trinity House, a very respected maritime authority in the United Kingdom, were at first sight not convinced as to the desirability of routing in the English Channel. When they saw that some form of routing was likely to be inevitable, they began to state the opinion that ships entering the North Sea should stay on the port or left hand side of the narrow waterway. This suited Trinity House's boarding stations for their pilots, but it ran against all the normally accepted maritime provisions whereby traffic keeps to the starboard or right-hand side of any channel.

So, the position was that the British Institute of Navigation was the leading authority in the International Association of Institutes of Navigation on this matter of channel routing, and here in the United Kingdom was a prestigious authority, Trinity House, indicating a solution to the problem which a number of us felt was, quite frankly, just wrong. I felt it appropriate to take a very strong line in the British Institute, to the effect that it was really most damaging to our general position that this prestigious body, Trinity House, looked upon as being a very significant nautical authority nationwide, should be taking a position which, firstly, was just wrong in all normal assumptions about the way in which traffic should be conducted and, secondly, a solution which wouldn't gain any support from any other part of the world. I am glad to say that the British Institute of Navigation was persuaded as to the sense of the views that I and a number of others had expressed. When we met the other countries to set up a voluntary arrangement for traffic separation at sea, it was done on the basis of having a separation zone, as it was called, in the middle of the Dover Strait, with traffic maintaining the right-hand side of the waterway into and out of the North Sea.

As I recall, I again tried to persuade the hydrographer, Steve Ritchie, to promulgate this information through the notices to mariners, but he still felt that it was purely a voluntary arrangement and it had no force of authority and it would be inappropriate for him to do this. Nevertheless, he was ready to take whatever action might be appropriate when the routing provisions could be given a greater degree of authority.

The practical outcome of the provisional routing arrangements which we had promulgated as far as we possibly could was very positive indeed. Reports came from huge numbers of ships, and inside Shell we conducted a survey of all the Masters of our own ships and ships we had in charter, as to what they thought of these temporary and voluntary routing arrangements. The results were very positive, there was a huge swell of opinion in the maritime world to the effect that routing in all sorts of areas was most highly desirable and should be pressed forward.

Two things happened as a result of this: one was that there were further meetings of the ad hoc group that had been set up to look at routing proposals. The group came up with a number of additional proposals for other parts of the world. Also, the International Maritime Consultative Organisation (IMCO), which was the governmental body, a specialist group operating under the auspices of the United Nations, took the matter on board and referred the principle of routing to its maritime safety committee. By this time, the practical effects of what had been done on a voluntary basis were so well understood and so well appreciated, there was absolutely no difficulty in IMCO reaching an early conclusion that routing was a very desirable matter. They decided it should be taken forward, the important area being the Hormuz Straits in the entrance to the Arabian Gulf.

I recall that this got me into some difficulties with the Executive Secretary of the Institute of Navigation who wanted the Institute to take matters further forward. I took the view, which I think was really indisputable, that once the matter had been taken up by the official body IMCO, the institutes of navigation could do no more than suggest any matters which they thought might be appropriate through the machinery of their governments. An important consideration was that once the routing provisions had effectively been given the seal of approval by the international body, Admiral Ritchie felt that he could then put all these proposals on his charts. This meant that routing was well understood and promulgated throughout the world.

I should record that after my retirement from Shell many years later, I joined the Northern Lighthouse Board as a co-opted commissioner. Trinity House were building a new tender for their lighthouse operations for our sister authority operating in English waters, and in my capacity as Chairman of the Northern Lighthouse Board I was invited to the naming ceremony of their new ship, *Patricia*, which was being named in the pool of London. The ship was very appropriately being named by Patricia, the daughter of Earl Mountbatten of Burma. The tour around the ship, and the reception afterwards in Trinity House, were being hosted by the Duke of Edinburgh in his capacity as Master of Trinity House. After the naming ceremony, the guests all assembled in the anteroom of Trinity House before lunch. I imagined that we would go and shake hands with our host, the Duke of Edinburgh, and then go and have a drink. However, when I went to go and shake hands with my host, with my wife by my side, he said, 'Dickson, I understand that you are now

Chairman of the Northern Lights'. I said that this was correct, and he said, 'Bloody stupid outfit that is. How can it be sensible to have a maritime authority largely run by a bunch of lawyers?' I was completely taken aback; I was not ready to defend the authority I was representing, and whilst I was aware at first sight that it did seem a little odd to have a maritime authority's governing body largely staffed by people whose background was a legal one, I knew from my experience of the Board of the Northern Lights that the Board functioned very satisfactorily. The history, as I understood it, of the way in which the board was constructed, was that when the Northern Lights were put in charge of an authority based in Edinburgh, it so happened that the only people with coastal responsibilities in Scotland meeting regularly in Edinburgh were the sherrifs, these being the Scottish equivalent of county court judges. Certainly, I have always been impressed with the sense of the American maxim, 'if it aint broke don't fix it'. In my opinion, the Northern Lights Board was working in a perfectly satisfactory way. Of course, the Trinity House people may have been somewhat disgruntled by the fact that previously the Northern Lights Board was required to take nautical advice from Trinity House, which was changed when certain sections of the merchant shipping act were rewritten in 1979 and co-option of people with nautical experience was required to be made to the Board. Indeed, my own co-option to the Northern Lights Board took place as a result of that change in the Act.

As I say, I was completely thrown by the attack by my host, and I am sorry to say, I said little to defend myself. However, having gone on at some considerable length about what he thought about the Northern Lights Board he then started on routing in the Channel: 'And another thing, Dickson, was that you were responsible for that stupid arrangement finally made for routing in the channel?' Here again, I was completely taken aback—I was not ready or in a position to defend myself. I was being attacked by my host, and there was nothing I could do about it. My poor wife was standing by my side wondering what was going to happen next. I suppose it is reasonable to assume that some of the elder brethren of Trinity House had been very much piqued by the attitude I personally had taken in the affairs of the Institute of Navigation; no doubt the discussions with the Deputy Master had reminded him that they had had this difficulty with me years and years before.

However, these things pass, and at the International Association of Lighthouse Authorities meeting in the United Kingdom, the Duke of Edinburgh in his capacity as Master of Trinity House hosted a reception for the delegates in the Guildhall. Feeling that I would possibly be attacked by my host on this occasion, I did brief myself very carefully both in the matter of the composition of the Board of the Northern Lights, and also on the history of routing arrangements in the Channel. However, my wife and I were received by our host on that occasion with extreme courtesy and there was no further discussion of these difficult matters.

The last thing I have to say on the matter of routing in the Channel is that, on my retirement from Shell in 1979, my marine colleagues were kind enough to present me with a framed copy of the admiralty chart of the Straits of Dover. This was signed by all the people in Shell who wished to come and attend my retirement party. It is one of my treasured possessions.

CHAPTER FIFTEEN

Board Responsibilities

I was elected to the Board of Shell International Marine on 1 January 1970. My interests and responsibilities didn't change to any great extent as a result of my election to the Board. The structure of Shell International Marine at that time was that we had a Managing Director who reported to the main Shell Board; we had a Director in charge of economics and finance, a Director in charge of chartering, a Director in charge of new construction and research development and my own responsibilities relating to operations and safety.

The responsibilities of Shell International Marine as a Company were to acquire and provide adequate tonnage to carry the Shell group of companies' oil, gas and chemicals in the most economically competitive way we possibly could. As far as the carriage of oil was concerned we owned roughly 50 per cent of the tonnage we operated, and 50 per cent we acquired on time charter. Time chartering a ship means that the owner gives to the charter full rights for employment of his ship, inside Shell International Marine we made little distinction between our own ships and the ships that we operated on time charter. In fact, I think it was very useful in the company to compare the performance of time chartered ships against the performance of ships owned by Shell companies.

As far as ships owned by Shell companies were concerned, the largest fleets were operated under the British and Dutch flags by Shell Tankers (UK) Ltd and Shell Tankers BV respectively. There were also substantial fleets of ships operated by French, German and Japanese companies. In the main, these ships were time chartered to Shell International Marine. In addition, a number of Shell companies around the world operated tankers for their internal trade. Shell International Marine offered advice to all these companies on the acquisition and operation of their ships. Once a year a marine conference was arranged in Shell Centre where all matters relating to the maritime transport of oil, gas and chemicals were discussed.

In Shell Marine at that time, we could claim that we were the largest maritime enterprise in the world. I consider myself to be extremely fortunate, since in my time in the marine side of Shell's operations I had with me people of high quality, I can't speak highly enough of the people who worked with me in my responsibilities. My part of the organisation was divided into three subdivisions, one headed by Captain Denis English, whom I regarded as my second in command. He was responsible for casualties which might occur either to owned ships or to ships in which we had cargo, that is time chartered ships, or voyage chartered ships. He also dealt with all the instructions sent out to ships on time charter, so that we could have a reasonably cohesive way of giving out the instructions to these ships. Another very difficult part of Captain English's responsibilities involved what we called tanker port performance. This meant keeping records of the efficiency with which ships loaded and discharged their cargoes. On the discharge part of the voyage especially, there were sophisticated means whereby the optimum performance of any ship in given circumstances could be determined, and then the actual performance of the ship against this optimum target was measured. Quite understandably, these matters sometimes led to a considerable amount of friction in the organisation, which the good Captain English bore with great fortitude.

Another subdivision, headed by Captain Lawrence, was responsible for the matters I have already described—the business of provision of adequate port facilities at loading and discharge terminals, and the scientific investigations necessary to ensure the most economical arrangements which could be provided. The third subdivision, headed by Maurice Oldsworth, who had an electrical engineering background, was responsible for marine safety and oil pollution. These were very important matters.

In addition to the carriage of crude oil and the various refined products around the world, Shell was widely involved in the carriage of chemicals and gas. Liquid petroleum gas had been carried for many years in pressurised vessels, in conventional tankers where the pressure kept the gas liquefied during carriage. Shell were very much in the forefront of the development of tankers which would work entirely differently. Essentially, this involved cooling the gas to a temperature where it would remain liquid at atmospheric pressure. With liquid natural gas or methane this involved cooling the liquid cargo to a temperature towards absolute zero. The liquid gas at this extremely low temperature was loaded into what was effectively a membrane tank of very sophisticated stainless steel, supported and insulated from the ship's hull by a wide range of balsa wood.

It was realised at this time that there was a very substantial quantity of liquid natural gas available in north Borneo, in Brunei. There was a very ready market for the gas in Japan; and this led to consideration being given as to how the gas could be loaded in a cryogenic state. One solution would obviously have been to build a harbour. This made me recall my early experience in Brunei, when we were trying to build a harbour for the tankers to export crude oil. However, the gas carriers now envisaged would be even bigger, so the costs involved in developing a harbour for these ships would be really enormous. Obviously, single buoy moorings would not be a solution to the problem, because the difficulties of putting cryogenic gas along a sea line and up through a swivel in a single buoy would be quite impossible to get round. It seemed to me, however, that we might well go back to the time-honoured means of loading tankers offshore in Borneo. This is where the oil was loaded over the stern of the ship, allowing the ship to move substantially one way, depending on the weather condition prevailing.

Joop Llangeveldt believed that he could build a crane, the purpose of which would be to carry the pipes to the ship. The problems involved in providing suitable moorings for the tankers were not very difficult to solve. However, the problems involved in providing the crane to carry the pipes to the afterend of the ship was a much more difficult problem to solve. I am glad to be able to say that Joop Llangeveldt and his people in the Dutch side of Shell, working with the contractors who were going to build this complicated crane, were able to solve all the problems. To date, an enormous amount of gas has been successfully sent to Japan in suitably built ships.

CHAPTER SIXTEEN

Oil Pollution

During the later years of my time in Shell, the difficulties resulting from pollution of coastal beaches and coastal waters by oil occupied a very considerable part of my working time. There were two aspects to this.

The first was what one might call operational oil pollution: that is, pollution occurring from the way in which tankers were operated. Over many years, the custom developed by tankers carrying crude or fuel oil cargoes was that, after discharge of their cargo and on the ballast voyage to the next loading port, the tanks would be cleaned. This was done to prevent the next cargo from being contaminated by residues. There could be between a half and one per cent of the total carrying capacity of the ship left over, which might contaminate the next cargo to be loaded. This problem meant that ships commonly washed out their tanks during the ballast voyage and discharged the washings directly to the sea. The effect of this was that in the parts of the world receiving substantial quantities of crude oil and exporting substantial quantities of refined black oil—that is, fuel oil and diesel—the beaches were continuously contaminated with the results of the washing out of the cargo tanks of the tankers leaving their discharge ports.

I came to the conclusion that if this washing out of the tanks could be avoided, it would help prevent a lot of discharge of oily waste. I managed to convince my marine colleagues that it would be perfectly possible to wash out the tanks so they could get ready for the next cargo, and avoid build up sludge on the bottom of the tanks which would make discharge difficult. I proposed that, instead of discharging the oily waste resulting from the washing process direct to the sea, they discharge it into a slop tank. The purpose of this would be to enable the oil to float on top of the water, then after the washing process of all the tanks, the water underneath the oil could be discharged leaving the oil residues in the ship.

I was easily able to convince my marine colleagues as to the sense and wisdom of this procedure, but those in the Shell organisation concerned with the refining operations were not so ready to believe us. It was quite obvious to them that the slop tank could never be completely drained of salt water; the next cargo to be discharged which would be loaded on top of the oil remaining in the slop tank would have contamination from perhaps a different grade of crude oil and also a certain amount of sea water.

However, a bonus was that there was a considerable amount of oil was actually saved with this system. Previously, the oil had been discharged in the sea, so if the refineries could deal with the problems of a certain amount of mixture of a different type of oil in their incoming cargoes and also the possibilities of a certain amount of sea water, they would reap the benefit of not losing around a half to one percent of the total oil to the sea. After some considerable practical experimentation, the refinery people became very enthusiastic about the possibility of their being able to deal with the problems that might arise from this new technique.

The government at this time were also very concerned about oil pollution and they had set up an oil pollution group chaired by a parliamentarian. My superiors in Shell believed that it would be timely and wise to inform this committee of the progress we had made in the direction of limiting what I call operational oil pollution. A meeting was arranged in the Shell boardroom, chaired by the then Managing Director with responsibility for marine affairs, one John Berkin. The chairman of the oil pollution committee was James Callaghan, later to be Prime Minister, and the secretary of the committee was Miss Barclay Smith, a lady who looked and behaved exactly like Joyce Grenfell.

John Berkin, who was a man of very considerable charm, had arranged to have Miss Barclay Smith sitting on his right hand. After he had opened the meeting with some preliminary words about our concern in the oil industry for oil pollution and how matters could be improved, he threw open the floor to the committee to make any observations they thought appropriate. Miss Barclay Smith had with her a sort of bead bag, from which she produced a very dead and very oiled guillemot, which she put on the boardroom table to emphasise the Royal Society for the Protection of Birds' interest in the matter. I thought that John Berkin handled the dead guillemot very effectively. He said, 'Miss Barclay Smith, it is really very good of you indeed to bring in this bird, which will emphasise to all of us the concern that your Society has about the effects of oil pollution on the sea birds around our coast lines; but, Miss Barclay Smith, you've obviously dirtied your hands bringing this bird out of its bag and we have adjacent to the boardroom a washroom and perhaps you would like to go and wash your hands.' Miss Barclay Smith said that she would, so he said, 'Well, perhaps it would be appropriate for you to put the guillemot back in your bag before you go, so that you won't dirty your hands when you come back.' So in no time flat he had achieved his objective of getting the guillemot off the boardroom table and back into the bag, and off went Miss Barclay Smith to wash her hands.

The meeting was successful in that we got a huge amount of encouragement from the committee in our efforts. It was obvious then that, in order to make the matter really effective, we would have to involve the American oil companies in similar operations. To this end, I was sent with a manufacturing colleague over to the United States to go around the offices of all the major American oil companies to explain what we had done and the results we had obtained. The American oil companies were at that time, after considerable pressure from the marine side of their Government, the United States Coastguard, very receptive. They were also intrigued by my refining colleagues' explanation about the amount of oil which would be recovered into the system by using this technique which became known as 'load on top'.

A different aspect of the oil company's problems relating to oil pollution was pollution of beaches and coastal waters following accidents to tankers resulting from collision or grounding. This type of pollution was most dramatically illustrated when a tanker, called the *Torey Canyon*, carrying a cargo for British Petroleum, went ashore on the Seven Stones rocks off the south-west coast of England, and spilt a substantial amount of Middle East crude oil into the sea. Huge areas of the Cornish beaches and surrounding coastal waters were affected. This was, in fact, the first time a major oil pollution of a coastline and surrounding coastal waters had occurred anywhere in the world. The British Government found themselves under enormous pressure to do something to ameliorate the situation.

After consultation, the government decided their best course of action would be to bomb the stricken vessel, hoping to set fire to the ship and her cargo and thereby reduce the amount of oil which might further escape from the ship. In the event, this proved to be a thoroughly unsatisfactory way of trying to deal with the problem. Some time later a select committee of the House of Commons was set up to look into the accident and the steps which had been taken to ameliorate the disaster. I was called before the select committee and asked my views about the decision to bomb and also what I thought might have been done as an alternative.

I had to say that, in my opinion, the decision to bomb the *Torey Canyon* did not have much chance of success. I did not believe it at all likely that much of the cargo could be set on fire by bombing the ship. I

141

considered that the likelihood was that if there was to be any extensive fire the probability was that it would burn off the light parts of the cargo, which would evaporate anyway and weren't going to cause pollution, whereas the heavier parts of the oil would remain and pollution would not be substantially prevented by the action taken.

When questioned as to what I considered might have been done as an alternative, I gave the opinion that a better option might well have been to put a small ship alongside the *Torey Canyon*. Then deep well pumps could have been used to pump the oil from the stricken tanker into the smaller ship, thereby reducing the amount of oil which might escape to the sea.

It so happened that I had an opportunity to put these ideas into practice, because a ship called *The Pacific Glory*, carrying a Shell cargo of crude oil up the Channel, was in collision with another ship. *The Pacific Glory* was badly damaged with fire at the afterend and driven ashore on the south coast of England. There were banner headlines in the newspapers the following morning, to the effect that once again the south coast of England was threatened with massive oil pollution. The oil industry, and Shell in particular this time, were getting a very bad press. I was able to put into practice the ideas that I had had about the possibility of putting a small ship alongside the stricken oil tanker, using deep well pumps to pump the oil out of the stricken ship into the smaller vessel.

The operation was undertaken and seemed to be going very well. In consultation with my PR colleagues in Shell, it was agreed that we should charter a helicopter and take some media people, both press and radio, to fly over the operation. We wanted to show them that there were successful ways of dealing with some accidents that might occur and it was felt that this would do some good for the oil industry in general, and perhaps Shell in particular. In the event, when we got over the two ships, to my surprise the media people didn't really seem to be at all interested. They weren't even very anxious to look out of the windows of the helicopter to see what was happening. When I asked the media people why they weren't showing any real interest in the operation they said, 'Well, this is the sort of thing that doesn't sell newspapers. If there were to be an explosion and one of the ships blew up then that would be a tremendous story, but you can't imagine that we are going to have a big headline to the effect that an operation is going on in the Channel which will be of no great interest to our potential readership.'

I well remember the cost of chartering the helicopter was £8,000. This seemed quite a sum of money at that time, and I remember being concerned that it had achieved absolutely nothing, either for the industry for which I was working, or for the company that was employing me. I had indeed over many years, in fact right up to my retirement from Shell, a good deal to do with the media in one way or another. I remember a very good piece of advice which a colleague and friend of mine on the PR side of Shell's activities gave me, which was that anybody can get their name into the newspapers or appear on television—the smart people are those who don't. This advice possibly stood me in good stead, because I remember on one occasion my wife and I had come up to Kenmore to do some salmon fishing for the spring salmon in the Tay system.

On the Sunday night when we had just arrived in the hotel, there was a telephone call for me and this was the BBC to say that they were going to have an item on the 'Panorama' programme on the Monday evening, which they wanted me to come and take part in. So I said, 'Well, I've got news for you—I've just started a week's salmon fishing, and there is absolutely no way that I'm going to come down to London on Monday.' So they said, 'We will run you down to Edinburgh and fly you down to London, and return you the following morning to Kenmore, and you will miss virtually nothing.' I said that they weren't hearing me—I wasn't coming, and that was the end of that. I was able to give them the name of another chap who I thought would be quite prepared to take it on, and he did—he got a terrible slating in the programme, and I felt that the advice I had had from my Shell PR colleague was a very good piece of advice indeed.

One of the very pleasant perks one had as a Director of Shell International Marine was that one's wife was invited to launch ships being built by ship owners for our time charter. The first ship my wife launched was a Canadian Pacific Tanker of about 45,000 tonnes to be launched in Rotterdam. She was by far the biggest ship this particular yard had ever built, and I don't know who was more nervous—the Chief Executive of the shipyard who had all the responsibilities of launching this very big ship into a very small channel, or my wife, who obviously had a certain amount of nervousness about performing the ceremony for the first time. Fortunately, everything went off very well indeed and it was a very pleasant occasion.

At that time, on the whole, ships were being built in dry dock. I think my wife was particularly fortunate in being asked to do three launches where a very large hull slides down into the water—it is a truly magnificent occasion—and I remember my wife saying that a launch is like a joyous birth, and a naming ceremony like a christening.

The second launch my wife did was a ship of somewhat similar size, called the *Gertrude Maersk*, which was being built for the Maersk line, a Danish shipping company. The operations director of this line and his wife had already, through business association, become quite close personal friends of ours, and it really was a quite delightful occasion. It was right in the middle of winter, I think it was in December—and the excitement and majesty of launching the ship was somewhat enhanced by the fact that at the time that the launch had to take place, because of the tide, the water into which the ship was going to slide was frozen to a depth of several inches of ice. Again for tidal reasons, the timing of the launch was quite late in the day; it was already getting dark, and I remember the children from the local town where the ship was being built had been invited to come and take part in the occasion. There was also a band from the local town; it was really splendid. When the ship finally went down the ways, huge slices of ice went slipping around all over the place, and there was a tremendous noise as the ship went into the water with its usual curtsey. Thereafter the launching party were invited to a quite magnificent dinner. As far as my wife and I were concerned, the pleasure was enhanced by the fact that all our children were invited to join the launching and the dinner.

The third launch my wife was asked to do was in San Diego, California. Here again we had a very close personal friend who was the Chief Executive of the company which owned the ship—the company was called Mormack Shipping. The Chief Executive was a friend called Jan Van Leer, who had been a Shell colleague of mine and had been a friend for many years. Once again the pleasure of the occasion was greatly enhanced by the fact that all our children were invited to join the launching party; whereas the Norwegian launch had been in bitterly cold weather with ice on the sea, the San Diego launch was the very opposite. It was a brilliantly hot day; the shipyard had brought a Mexican band along, and it was a splendid occasion with flags flying, bands playing and the ship sliding down majestically into beautifully clear blue water.

After the launch, the company receiving the ship gave a magnificent dinner party in the hotel in which we were all staying. My wife had the rather formidable task of making a speech, which she did very well and it was very well received. The following evening, the yard which had built the ship gave a reception in a passenger liner moored in the harbour of San Diego—this was another splendid occasion.

A very important and very taxing part of my responsibilities was dealing with casualties which might occur either to ships owned by Shell companies or to ships in which Shell cargoes were being carried. This brought me into contact with salvage contractors around the world, the most noted of these being a Dutch company called Smitt which I had a great deal to do with. I was really very fortunate, in that I didn't really have any problems with my superiors, because quite large sums of money could be involved in salvage operations. However, my superiors took the view that decisions had to be made and somebody had to make them, and I was in that position. I really had a very free hand—I could either negotiate a deal with a salvage company to provide towage for a ship on a daily rate basis, or I could negotiate a salvage contract on what was known as Lloyds open form. Lloyds open form as a salvage contract is a wonderful document which has stood the test of time. Essentially, the contract places an onus on the salvage contractor to take charge of the ship and get the ship into a place of safety. The salvage contractor enters into the agreement on a basis of *no cure no pay*.

When a ship is in trouble there are three elements at risk. There is the ship herself, the cargo and the freight—that is, the money to be paid for the carriage of the cargo. The contract provides that, when the ship has been delivered to a place of safety in due time and away from the dreadful problems that confront those involved in the operation, care can be taken to estimate the value of the three elements: the value of the ship, the value of the cargo and the value of the freight. Account can then be taken of the skill and expertise deployed by the salvage contractor to get the ship to a place of safety. The parties to the contract agree that the value of the salvage award divided in proportion to the relative value of the salvage elements will be subject to arbitration. In many cases, after a successful salvage, the parties agree to the salvage award and the division of costs between the ship, the cargo and the freight. If they cannot agree then the Lloyds arbitrator, a Queen's Counsel—a very experienced barrister of the Admiralty Court—is called in, and he can arbitrate. The arbitration is, of course binding on all the parties.

As I have said, the Lloyds open form has stood the test of time, and has a very high reputation in the whole of the maritime world. However, a complication arose when oil pollution became a problem, because large tankers carrying huge quantities of polluting oil could get into the situation where the ship would be very badly damaged. Some of the cargo may have been lost, so that the salvage effort that would have to be deployed by a salvage contractor would not be adequately compensated by the value of cargo recovered by the salvage operation. However, at the same time, the cost of third party damage due to oil pollution and the cost of clean-up might still represent a considerable amount of money.

When we had a casualty in Shell, Denis English and I used to call together a body which became known as the Troika. It consisted of the lawyer in Shell with responsibilities for marine, the executive in the company responsible for insurance matters, and an average adjuster whom we retained, since he was an expert in salvage awards and salvage matters generally. We thought long and hard about the problem of a ship being in terrible danger and not being an attractive proposition for a salvage contractor, but still posing a huge oil pollution risk. We came to the conclusion that the time honoured advantages of Lloyds open form should, if possible, be retained. We thought, however, that there should be another element introduced into the form which would deal with the potential cost liabilities for oil pollution damage and clean-up.

We had very extensive exploratory discussions with Lloyds, and also with representatives of the protection and indemnity clubs,—that is, the insurance arrangements whereby ship owners seek to insure their third party liabilities. I was invited to present a paper on the subject to a salvage conference which took place in New York in 1979, attended by a wide section of both the oil industry and salvage contractors. The views I put forward were received with considerable approval. I am glad to say that, eventually, the Lloyds open form was modified to take account of this oil pollution difficulty.

I have already mentioned that I had considerable freedom concerning what should be done with a ship in difficulties. I imagine that in most British companies similar arrangements applied; somebody in the company would be given responsibility to take whatever decisions had to be taken.

Towards the end of my time in Shell, a very strange accident occurred. A ship called the *Amoco Cadiz*, belonging to an American oil company based in Chicago, and carrying a cargo on exchange for Shell suffered damage in very severe weather in the English Channel. The damage amounted to the complete loss of the connection of the ship's rudder to the steering engine controlling the rudder. This meant, of course, that the ship was completely unmanoeuvrable. She ended up heading towards the coast of Brittany. Strangely enough, she began to make very slow but steady progress towards the coast of Brittany, the strong winds blowing up-channel acting on the side of the tanker like the sails of a ship, and driving her like a sailing ship towards the shore. Smitt's, who always know what is going on in the world of distress, had a tug deployed and offered a Lloyds open form salvage contract. If the ship had been a time chartered ship carrying a Shell cargo, she would have had our Shell instructions telling the Master that we, as time chartered, would be very happy for him to conclude a salvage agreement on the basis of Lloyds open form.

146

However, the *Amoco Cadiz* had no such instruction, and the Master of the ship referred to his superiors in the Chicago head office. Apparently, in American commercial life every executive in a company has an amount of money which he can commit, and to commit a sum of money beyond his authorisation is regarded as a very serious commercial blunder. So, when the Master asked permission from his owners in Chicago to conclude a salvage agreement the first question asked was, 'What is the value of the contract?' The only contract that Smitts would entertain was a contract on Lloyds open form. The value of this would only be determined in the event when the ship and cargo were delivered to a place of safety, and all the procedures necessary to determine a reasonable amount of money to be paid to the contractor could be quantified. No one in the Chicago office was prepared to accept responsibility for an unquantified sum of money. So the ship slowly but surely drifted towards the shore, and eventually went to shore on the Brittany coast causing widespread oil pollution damage. Shell, in France, received some serious adverse publicity relating to the accident. Certainly, I and my marine colleagues were most unpopular with our French counterparts, but the accident had already happened. With hindsight, it is very difficult to see what could have been done to improve the circumstances of the accident.

Certainly, we spent a great deal of time struggling with various possibilities for reducing the effects of these severe degrees of oil pollution. One possibility we investigated was the idea of a ship being fitted with buoyant arms sticking out into the sea, forming an approximate right angle. The ship would be driven along, and would effectively funnel the oil into a reception area where it could be treated in a manner not dissimilar to 'load on top'. A prototype small vessel was built, which worked very well in quiet water, but was completely useless as soon as there was any wave action. Similar difficulties arose with the concept of booms, which it was thought might be designed and placed around pollution in the sea. Once again, this had some value in quiet water but proved to be quite useless where there was any substantial wave action.

A considerable amount of thought was given to the possibility of a technique which became known as 'sand sink'. The idea was that a dredger would be used to scoop up sand from a suitable sandy area of the sea bed. The sand would be coated with silicon, which would make it stick to oil, and then the dredger could be taken out to an area of the sea polluted by oil and spray the coated sand onto the oil. The effect of this would be to make the oil non-buoyant, so it would sink to the bottom of the sea like a carpet. It worked to an extent, but there were two serious difficulties. Firstly, the oil like a black carpet on the sea bed was likely to do just as much damage—perhaps more damage—than oil floating on the surface, which eventually does get broken up by the action of wind and waves. That, in fact, was the second disadvantage—the oil on the sea bed remained practically intact after the sand sink operation, and wasn't destroyed by the normal action of the sea.

The last method for dealing with oil slicks on the sea's surface was to spray the oil with suitable chemicals. This is the action which is now normally taken to disperse the oil. It does reduce the amount of pollution of coastal waters, but it is arguable whether the damage done by the chemicals used to disperse the oil is not greater than the damage which might be done by the oil itself. Indeed, these considerations led me to speculate as to whether it was desirable to spray oil with chemicals at all, except in areas of particularly cold water where the natural breakdown of the oil is very much retarded.

Another aspect of oil pollution requiring attention was the means whereby money could be made available for clean-up after a tanker accident causing oil pollution. After lengthy discussions in the oil industry with the time-honoured ship owners' third party insurance arrangements, the protection and indemnity clubs, it was agreed that a new contract should be drawn up known as 'the tanker owner's voluntary acceptance of liability for oil pollution', with the acronym TOVALOP. It became obvious, however, that the monetary limits of liability set for TOVALOP might not in all cases meet the costs which could follow third party liabilities and clean-up costs after major tanker accidents. The oil industry, after much discussion, came to the conclusion that there should be a second fund. The maritime part of the oil industry eventually agreed to set up an arrangement which became known as the Crystal Contract. This Crystal arrangement would meet claims and costs for clean-up beyond that which might be met by the TOVALOP arrangements.

At the same time all these matters were receiving the attention of the International Maritime Consultative Organisation, headquartered in London, where the maritime parts of governments around the world meet to discuss all matters relating to marine accidents. Another matter of serious concern to the oil industry, and also to the International Maritime Consultative Organisation, was the general safety of tankers carrying crude oil cargoes, and in particular the risks involved in cleaning tanks. This was brought into sharp focus by an accident to a Shell tanker of 200,000 tonnes dead weight. The tanker, *Mactra*, was undergoing the tank cleaning operations while proceeding northward on her voyage to the Persian Gulf to load, and had rounded the Cape of Good Hope, when there was a very severe explosion in one of the tanks being cleaned. A detailed investigation was soon underway, to determine firstly, why the accident had happened and secondly, what measures should be taken to avoid a recurrence. The way in which tanks were cleaned during the ballast voyage was that a Butterworth machine, which was rather like an enormous garden sprinkler, was lowered into the tank and sea water was pumped at high pressure through this sprinkler. Investigations showed that it was possible, in certain conditions, that effects not entirely dissimilar to the formation of thunderclouds could take place in the huge compartments of these ships during the cleaning operation. Thus, it had to be expected that there could be circumstances where an electrical discharge could take place in the tank, which would give rise to an explosion. Hydrocarbon gas in any enclosed compartment will only explode when the proportion of hydrocarbon gas to oxygen is at a certain proportion. Prior to the *Mactra* accident, it had been confidently assumed that during the tank cleaning operation the atmosphere in the tank would normally be over rich, that is the proportion of hydrocarbon gas compared to oxygen would be greater than that which could give rise to an explosion. The *Mactra* accident proved this was not always the case.

Some parts of the tanker industry had been experimenting for some time with arrangements whereby the tank atmosphere would be made inert. This was done by taking the flue gas, mainly carbon dioxide, from the ship's propulsion machinery, and injecting the gas into the tanks. I was convinced that this not only enhanced the safety during the tank cleaning operations, but it enhanced the safety of a ship during the whole of her trading activities. I am glad to say that I was able to convince my colleagues in Shell that we should convert all our ships to the inert gas system, and this was done.

There was a growing realisation in the marine part of the oil industry that all these matters needed consultation. This included suitable and sensible liaison with governmental authorities and also with the International Maritime Consultative Organisation. So a body called the Oil Companies International Marine Forum was set up with responsibility to look after the single buoy mooring form, the TOVALOP arrangements, Crystal, liaison with governments and with the International Maritime body. I had a seat on the board of the OCIMF, and for the two years immediately prior to my retirement from Shell I was its Chairman.

The companies with responsibilities for the administration of the TOVALOP and Crystal contract were Bermudan registered companies.

Bermuda demands that board meetings have to take place in Bermuda, at reasonably regular intervals, and that there have to be Bermudan directors on the boards of the various companies registered in Bermuda. I remember Bermuda as a very beautiful island; it was the final staging post in flights back to the United Kingdom from the Caribbean, and I spent quite a few nights there in my early days. As the years went past it became a very popular American holiday resort, with the result that eventually, to my mind, Bermuda became a sort of Blackpool in the middle of the Atlantic. However, as I have said, the various directors of the companies registered in Bermuda used to meet there regularly. Of course, it was very pleasant, because my wife and I became very friendly with a number of the representatives of the other companies. We found a relatively small, but very comfortable hotel on the other side of the main harbour from Hamilton, the capital of Bermuda, and we had some very happy times there.

Our last visit to Bermuda was the occasion of my retirement from the Chairmanship of the Board of the OCIMF, which coincided with the retirement of the then Chief Executive of the Crystal organisation. Our friends and colleagues gave us a very splendid retirement dinner party, at which I was presented with four delightful engravings. One was of my home town, Edinburgh, another of Greenock, where I had served in a destroyer for quite a considerable part of the war. A third was of the Island of Arran and the fourth was of what was then known to be our retirement home in Perthshire. I am afraid that one of the difficulties about one's friends being spread around the world is that on retirement you don't see very much of them, but these engravings are a very treasured possession. I often look at them and think of the friends we had, our meetings and discussions about the various problems with which we had to struggle.

CHAPTER SEVENTEEN

Problems Near to Home

Shell were in the forefront of the oil industry in acquiring and operating enormous tankers of 200,000 tonnes dead weight and above. The operation of these ships carrying Middle East crude to north-west Europe was complicated by the fact that our main discharge port in north-west Europe, Rotterdam, could not take these ships fully laden. One of our competitor companies, confronted with the same problem, decided to build a reception port in the South of Ireland, in Bantry Bay, where these ships could be discharged and the cargo loaded into smaller ships which would feed their refineries. It was generally accepted in the oil industry that the transfer from ship to ship of highly volatile Middle East crude cargoes should not be undertaken, except in very special circumstances and in very quiet sheltered water. However, I remembered in my early days as a lecturer in Leith Nautical College I had in my class a number of Norwegians. They were experienced in the whaling industry in the Antarctic and they had described to me how dead whales could be used as fenders. They were extremely efficient in keeping the largest whale factory ships and their supply tankers safe in relatively nasty weather conditions in the Antarctic. It seemed to me that, if we could produce fenders which would have characteristics similar to whales, it might be possible to transfer oil from ship to ship in the English Channel. I discussed the problem with a man called Bennett Burleigh who had supplied us with anchors and cables and other marine equipment, and who had a small yard in the Clyde. He said that he could find a solution to the problem which would involve using ten-foot diameter tyres from large earth-moving vehicles. These enormous tyres, inflated to their normal operating pressure, would be mounted on a steel tube on suitable bearings which would allow them to revolve. We called them whale fenders; two of these whale fenders were thought to be sufficient to protect the two tankers, lying in open water, from collision. Collision between the two ships could conceivably cause a spark; if there were to be any spillage of highly volatile crude oil this could create a very dangerous situation.

At that time, the ships that we were using to carry the crude oil from the Middle East were ships of just over 200,000 tonnes dead weight. The ship we proposed to use for the lightening operation was a tanker of 70,000 tonnes dead weight, one of the D class of ships. I was convinced that the way to do the operation was to have the large ship steaming on a pre-determined course at very slow speed. Then the D class ship, modified to carry the whale fenders, could steam slowly on a parallel course, slowly converging with the bigger ship; then lines could be fired over to the large ship from the 70,000 tonne tanker using what were called costain guns.

My PR colleagues in Shell were very worried about the possible side-effects of these operations being carried out off the south coast of England. After the accident to the *Torey Canyon*, there was still a considerable amount of concern about the possibility of oil pollution on the coast line. The area we envisaged using on the south-west coast of England was Lyme Bay, which is an area very conveniently sheltered from the prevailing westerly winds. We had in mind that, if the wind was in the south, we could do the operation on the French side of the Channel under the shelter of the Cherbourg peninsula. My PR colleagues arranged a meeting in the West Country, which was attended by all the local members of parliament representing the west of England constituencies, together with various dignitaries from local councils and the Ministry of Transport people with in charge of marine safety.

We were perhaps fortunate in that one or two of the people who attended the meeting were people I had known in my naval days. They were quite helpful in giving their opinion that what we were proposing to do seemed to them, with their naval experience, to be quite well thought out and a thoroughly sensible operation. However, the government decided that, before they could give their *carte blanche* to what we were proposing, we would have to carry out an operation attended by their professional people. We were to put the two ships together and transfer water from one to the other, instead of oil. So we did an experiment with a Dutch 200,000 tonner coming on her way in ballast back to the Middle East. We put the 70,000 tonne ship alongside with all the government dignitaries on board; the operation went perfectly smoothly, and after that there was no further opposition and the operations went ahead with crude oil.

I recall that, in the first year of operations, it was estimated that the company saved somewhere in the order of nine million pounds. This was quite a lot of money in those days, and was due to the way in which we had been able to load the ships to full draught and deal with the crude oil. The 70,000 tonne ship was able to take off enough oil to allow the

200,000 tonne ship to get into Rotterdam. I remember that I was given a bonus of several hundred pounds, which I was very pleased with, and that enabled us to buy a dinghy. This was something I particularly wanted to do, because I wanted the children to learn how to sail.

The family had quite a lot of fun with the dinghy. We used to sail it quite a bit in the Thames, and occasionally we took it down to the south coast. Every year we used to take it up to the Island of Arran, where the family went for the summer holiday.

The size of tanker used for carrying crude oil from the Middle East was increasing. Shell were planning to build a class of 300,000 tonne ships, and our French marine company were planning to own two tankers of 500,000 tonnes dead weight. So thought had to be given to even deeper water facilities to discharge these huge ships in north-west Europe. One of the Shell refineries taking a considerable amount of oil for distribution around the United Kingdom was Stanlow. The tanker berth at Tranmere, which was where crude oil ships could be discharged to the refinery at Stanlow, had been designed for ships of around 60,000 tonnes dead weight. It seemed to be quite impossible ever to cater for ships of 300,000 and eventually 500,000 tonnes dead weight in the River Mersey. So, thought was given to the possibility of laying a single buoy mooring off the North Wales coast to connect to Stanlow refinery by pipeline. The depth of water there readily available quite reasonably close to the shore would cater for ships of any conceivable size in the future. At that time, however, the idea of having a single buoy mooring in unsheltered water had not been tried anywhere in north-west Europe, and there was obviously going to be a considerable amount of potential hostility to the ideas we were beginning to develop.

The site that we chose was off a small town called Amlwch on the North coast of the Isle of Anglesey. We had at this time made a film in Shell about our single buoy moorings in other parts of the world. My PR colleagues felt that it would be a good thing to start by calling a meeting in Anglesey which would be attended by all the local interested parties. This would let us explain the idea of single buoy moorings and develop the reasons why we wanted to put one off the coast of the Island of Anglesey. This would offset any possible difficulties in the early stages. In the event, the meeting was attended by some very hostile people who elected a chairman to open the proceedings, which he did in the Welsh language. This was a slight difficulty, because none of us, who were going to make our exposition of our plans understood what he was saying. However, we showed the film, and I gave an exposition of what we were planning to do and the reasons for it, and why it would be a good thing for Anglesey. Our plan was to have a small port authority formed; this would have revenue from the ships, which would be good for them, and good for the country as a whole. I couldn't have been very convincing in my arguments, because at the end of my exposition a chap at the back of the hall stood up and said, 'You are a bloody liar.'

However, it was decided that we should press ahead with the project. The chosen route was to promote a private bill through the House of Lords. Their Lordships' house decided to set up a committee to listen to the arguments for and against the project being contemplated. This committee was chaired by a noble lord called Royal who had been, I understand, a Labour whip at some previous time. He had five peers sitting with him on his committee and he called evidence from Shell to explain what we were going to do, what we thought the risks were, and how we proposed to deal with any problems that might arise. He then took evidence from the various people who were objecting to the proposals. There were representatives from Friends of the Earth, who said that they thought there was a risk of oil pollution which was quite unacceptable.

In the evidence I gave to the committee I tried to allay the fears about oil pollution, largely on the grounds that crude oil had to be supplied to this large refinery, and it could be supplied in one of two ways. Either we could take it through a single buoy mooring off the coast of Anglesey, or we could take it into the Mersey. I argued that the risks of taking oil into the Mersey river were greater, in my opinion, than the single buoy mooring risks. I recall that one of the objectors was the Marquis of Anglesey who, I think, didn't endear himself entirely to the chairman of the committee by appearing before the committee in his shooting attire. When the chairman asked him what his objections were, he explained that there were very valuable marshes around the Welsh coast in the vicinity of the proposed single buoy mooring site; he felt that oil pollution in that area would seriously affect very valuable duck shooting. I recall that Lord Royal said, 'Yes, my noble Lord of Anglesey, but what makes you think that ducks would rather be shot than coated in bloody oil?'

In the event, the House of Lords passed the bill, and the proposals went ahead. The single buoy mooring was quite successful, although I understand that long after my retirement from Shell the oil was coming in from Shetland. The very big ships that had been used were not needed any more and I understand that the whole project has now been shelved.

Shell had another large project in view at this time; this was the landing of methane gas from the fields in the North Sea. The gas would be liquefied and loaded as cryogenic liquid into tankers, and my colleagues on the production side of the business had chosen Peterhead as the harbour most convenient to their plans for landing the gas on the north-east coast of Scotland. The harbour at Peterhead is really very interesting. It was originally built by prisoners taken during the Napoleonic wars, the purpose of the harbour was as a harbour of refuge. The coast of Scotland north of Aberdeen is a particularly formidable and hostile coast for fishermen and small craft; the idea was that Peterhead would be a harbour of refuge in the nasty weather that can often be experienced in the wintertime off that coastline. The sheltered water for the harbour of refuge was made by throwing a stone breakwater out from the southern part of the town of Peterhead. The breakwater was substantially improved as the years went by, by prisoners from the prison at Peterhead. It is quite interesting that if one walks along the breakwater you can see where the fellows who laid the huge granite blocks to make the breakwater have carved their initials, and in some cases their names, and the dates that they were working on the jetty.

Plans had already been laid at that time for a tanker berth at the south end of the jetty, at the protecting breakwater, for tankers discharging fuel oil. The plans for the gas tankers were that they would lie at the northern end of the breakwater. Obviously, before a project of this type could go ahead, there would have to be a public enquiry. Shell retained the services of the then Dean of the Faculty of Scottish Advocates, one James McKay, now the Lord Chancellor.

About this time, a great deal of work was being done in the industry concerning safety aspects of the loading and carriage of cryogenic gas. Shell perhaps being, at that time, the company with the greatest exposure to this type of cargo, took a very leading part in all these matters. Perhaps the most important aspect of the work undertaken was the thought given to what would happen if the outer hull and the inner container in the tanker of the cryogenic gas at these terribly low temperatures were to be punctured due to grounding or collision. It was realised that the liquid gas would immediately vaporise; a cloud of gas would form which could move in the wind, and if a certain proportion of gas to oxygen in the air occurred, ignition would cause a violent explosion. This led to acceptance of the fact that extreme care had to be taken in circumstances where tankers of this type were to be accommodated, loaded and discharged. It was agreed that they must be, as far as possible, safe from either the possibility of a collision or a grounding.

Extensive discussions between the marine part of Shell, intent on achieving the highest possible degree of safety for these ships, and our Dutch counterparts in Holland responsible for the design of the berth, led to a conclusion that it would be very difficult, if not impossible, to provide adequate safety arrangements in the harbour at Peterhead. It was known that in violent weather, particularly weather from the south-east, the breakwater at Peterhead could be washed over by waves at high water. This meant that the tanker lying in the proposed area of the berth would be subject to quite violent wave action, with the risk of the possibility of failure of the mooring arrangements.

My civil engineering colleagues in the Dutch side of the business undertook to run model tests, to see whether anything could be done to relieve the dangers. They did this by building up what would effectively be a sand bank, a bank of material, on the outside of the jetty—the effect of this would be to break the wave action. It was found that, whilst the situation could be improved, the ship in the berth would still be subject to violent movement due to the residual wave action. The conclusion to which I came was that it was just not an acceptable risk, my strong advice to my colleagues on the production side of the business was that they should abandon their plans for loading arrangements at Peterhead. I recommended they take a pipeline down through Scotland to the Firth of Forth, where the conditions for a berth would be, to my mind, entirely satisfactory. My production colleagues didn't like this advice at all. They considered that the costs of moving from Peterhead to the Firth of Forth would be much higher, and they said that surely it must be possible in deteriorating circumstances to take the ship out of the berth and out of the harbour. To my mind this was a completely unacceptable possible arrangement. I could envisage a situation where a substantial part of the crew of the ship might be ashore, and in deteriorating weather they would say, 'Oh well, it'll be all right, we'll be OK', and before they could make up their mind to take the ship away from the jetty and out to the open sea, the situation would deteriorate to an extent where it would be a dangerous operation to try to leave the berth and go through the entrance to the harbour.

In the event, a serious difference of opinion developed between the production people, whose concern it was to get the most cost effective means of exporting their gas, and the marine people—supported, I am glad to say, by the civil engineers, who said it was really impossible to build an adequately safe harbour. The matter went, of course, to the main Shell board; the managing directors really felt that they had no alternative but to accept the views of those of us who felt that there was a doubt about the safety of the project. In the event, it was decided to take the gas to the Firth of Forth. As far as I was concerned, it was a very happy outcome because the Forth ports authority, a properly constituted body, were very happy to make arrangements to ensure the highest possible degree of safety for ships coming into the terminal on the north side of the Firth of Forth at a place called Braefoot Bay. There, completely sheltered jetties could be built where the ship would be completely safe against any possibility of serious weather resulting in mooring failures. In the event, our partners in the venture, Esso, who had title to 50 per cent of the methane being produced, found that the facility of the pipeline coming down to that part of Scotland was very convenient for them because they wanted to use the methane as chemical feedstock.

CHAPTER EIGHTEEN

Retirement

Shortly before my retirement from Shell, I attended a Shell evening function in Shell Centre. I found myself sitting next to a previous chairman of Shell Transport and Trading, Sir David Barron. Sir David said that he felt that one of the sensible things to do in retirement was to take jobs which were not necessarily financially rewarded, but which were interesting. He said that as long as one's expenses were covered, it was a very reasonable thing to accept office where one could use one's knowledge to help some particular body.

I was fortunate in that, at the time of my retirement, there was a lot of consideration given to the Northern Lights Board. Scotland, at that time, was flexing some independence muscle. It was agreed that the Northern Lights Board, which had previously sought advice on nautical matters from Trinity House, should no longer need to do that. Instead, someone with nautical experience was to be appointed to the board, and I was asked to join the Northern Lights Board. I found my responsibilities on the board both interesting and rewarding. In fact, I served on the board until 1994, a total of 15 years.

My colleagues in Shell thought that I would be back in a few months looking for further employment. On retirement one does get offers, I had several offers which would have been financially rewarding, but all of them would have involved travelling. My wife and I had agreed that when I retired we would spend time together, so I could see absolutely no point in taking on further work which would mean a huge amount of travelling around the world.

My wife, looking after my wellbeing and interests as she always had, arranged with a Norwegian shipowner friend of ours that on my retirement he would provide a voyage down to South Africa on one of his tankers which was going around the Cape to load crude oil in the Middle East. The idea was that we would helicopter off the ship to Cape Town and spend as long as we wanted there; when we were ready to come back we could helicopter back onto one of his ships going the other way and come back to the United Kingdom. In fact, we spent a month going around the Cape. We hired a little car, and it was a great pleasure for me to show my wife parts of the Cape which I had known during my naval service time when we were running convoys around the Cape from Cape Town to Durban. It is one of the most beautiful parts of the world I have ever seen.

Shell, as a company, always had the best interests of their staff clearly in view. They arranged a retirement course for people just before retirement, which my wife and I both attended. On that course people were advised that it was not a very good idea to leave one's place of domicile on retirement, because you would be leaving behind friends that you had made. They said that going to a strange place which you might have visited on holiday and which seemed idyllic as a holiday location could be quite different when you went to stay there permanently. However, my wife and I are both Scots, and we had always planned that we would return to Scotland. After much thought, we decided that there was a lot to be said for central Perthshire. To some extent, this was a compromise, because my wife had always been attracted to the west coast of Scotland, whereas I had had a lot of interest and pleasure in the east coast. Perthshire, of course, is in the middle. We agreed that we would take this step, and that if either of us felt that we had done the wrong thing, then we wouldn't be proud and we would admit we had made a mistake and go back down south again.

In the event, we were fortunate to find a house in a place called Kenmore, a small village at the eastern end of Loch Tay. We have been very happy here, and it has been an ideal place for our children and grandchildren to come and visit. Our Swedish son-in-law, who is a super chap, decided that he was going to build a Swedish log house about four miles from where we stay in Kenmore. He made it available to other members of the family, so we have the great delight of having our family able to come and join us every year during the summer months, and they can use the log house when the Swedish part of the family are not using it. This is an ideal arrangement for them and for us.

I was asked by the Liberian Bureau of Marine Affairs to act as investigating officer, sitting with an assessor, to look into the explosion which had happened in one of their registered ships. This ship was called the *Albahaa*; she was a very large crude carrying tanker and was destroyed following an explosion with considerable loss of life off the east coast of Africa on 3 April 1980. I approached this commission with some trepidation, because I've always feared the difficulties that relate to sitting in judgement on one's fellow men. I was concerned that I might have to take very serious action if there should have been any dereliction of duty prior to, or as a contributing cause to the explosion and the loss of the ship. I've always believed in the maxim, 'there but for the grace of God go I.' The investigations were held in the Liberal Club in London and went on for almost a week. There was at that time a growing body of knowledge in the industry about what had happened in the tank of the tanker, during the cleaning operations after carriage of a volatile crude oil cargo. It appeared that what had happened to this unfortunate ship was that the tank-cleaning operations, which involved lowering into the tank a piece of equipment rather like an enormous garden sprinkler, had generated a cloud in the tank not dissimilar to a thunder cloud. In certain circumstances, this cloud could be discharged—effectively, this would be rather like a lightning discharge inside the tank; if at the same time there were to be an explosive mixture either in the whole or a significant part of the tank, then a huge explosion would result. Fortunately this is a very rare combination of circumstances; the *Albahaa* was just extremely unfortunate. I was able to report that no serious blame should be attached to any of the ship's company for the accident which had occurred. This was a very happy outcome as far as I was concerned, because I have always taken the view that for people engaged in the sort of business I was in,—the transport business: shipping, trains, aircraft, etc—where an accident occurs causing death or serious injury, and following an investigation if people are held to blame, it must be a really dreadful thing to carry through one's life. I can remember mistakes which I made and which, fortunately, didn't result in a serious accident, I regard myself as being very fortunate.

I was also asked by Gulf Oil to act as an expert witness in a case which had been brought against them by the owners of a ship, which had had an accident at their single buoy mooring terminal off the west coast of Africa. They asked me what I thought would be appropriate in the way of fees for my undertaking this on their behalf. I said that I didn't really want any remuneration, because tax at that time was punitive, but I would like, if I was involved at all, to be able to take my wife to wherever there might be a hearing—on the other side of the Atlantic as it was anticipated at that time—and I asked for first class travel at their expense for myself and my wife. They readily agreed to this, and we did go across to Philadelphia, where we had some friends. It was a very pleasant visit as we were able to look up these old friends. I am glad to say that after a preliminary hearing with the lawyers of both sides of the case, the Gulf's opponents agreed to drop their claim.

Another job which I undertook was to join the Pilotage Committee which had been set up by the government to look into pilotage matters in the United Kingdom. I had always been interested in pilotage and had, in fact, been chairman of the Pilotage Committee of the General Council of Shipping. I found that these duties, together with the considerable amount of work I had with the Northern Lights Board, was taking up rather more of my time than I wanted. My long-suffering wife was beginning to get a bit upset about the amount of time I was spending away from home, so I resigned from the Pilotage Commission.

I did, however, stay on as a commissioner of the Northern Lighthouses. I found this very interesting for two reasons. One was that, as a navigator, I was very interested in the changes that were happening in the navigational world due to considerable advances in electronic aids of all kinds. Also, my colleagues on the board looked to me to take a considerable part in the management and running of the lighthouse tenders. When I joined the board there were three tenders used for supply of equipment to the various lighthouses around the coast of Scotland. We were then reduced to two ships; both of them were getting fairly old and I was anxious that the board should acquire a new vessel. I had great difficulty in persuading the government to build. At that time, the government officials with whom we were dealing were under instruction from their political masters that no expense should be undertaken unless it was absolutely necessary. Regretfully, we missed what I would regard as being a good opportunity to build. This meant that I had to stay on, as my colleagues on the board were particularly anxious that I should not resign until I had got the ship designed and built for their requirements. The long-term objective was that if we could build a really efficient new ship it might well be that we could reduce from two ships to one which would result in considerable savings.

Commissioners of the Northern Lighthouses undertake to serve in three year terms; all this meant that I took a three year term longer than my wife thought appropriate. My objectives were that the new ship should be in accordance with all the modern design improvements which would enable her to operate as efficiently as possible around the coast of Scotland. I wanted the ship to be built, preferably, in a Scottish yard, but if not in Scotland then certainly somewhere in the United Kingdom. I thought it crazy to build a ship for a quasi-governmental body in the Far East, which is exactly what our sister authority, Trinity House, had done. Finally, I wanted the ship to be a nice-looking vessel that people would be proud and happy to serve in. I am glad to say that all these objectives were, I believe, realised. We had a very happy occasion where Her Majesty The Queen graciously agreed to launch the new ship, which was built in Ferguson's Yard in Port Glasgow. We had the great pleasure of entertaining Her Majesty to lunch after the launching.

RETIREMENT

I was asked to become an honorary Sheriff of the Perth Court, an office which I was honoured to accept. I undertook to chair the tribunal which heard appeals from people who thought that their housing or business rating had been wrongly judged by the rating authority. I also undertook to act as the emergency planning officer for the district. Central government had instructed all local authorities to set up arrangements whereby people could be appointed to co-ordinate action should there be a dire emergency. What I think they had in mind was the awful prospect of a nuclear holocaust. I found this quite interesting, because one had to envisage what would happen in the relatively remote part of Scotland where we live if petroleum and electricity were suddenly to be denied. I soon came to the conclusion that if one looked upon survival as being simply a matter of feeding, shelter and warmth then we, in this part of the world, could exist perhaps not comfortably, but we could survive perfectly easily for quite a long time. In fact, it seemed to me that perhaps our greatest problem would be to deal with an influx of people from the cities where conditions, in terms of survival, would probably be very much more difficult. Happily, the prospect of a dreadful catastrophe has very much receded. I haven't heard anything about emergency planning over a number of years, and I imagine that I am now absolutely and completely retired.

Epilogue

I consider myself to be extremely fortunate in that I have had a wonderful life. I wouldn't regard my service in the Navy in wartime as being entirely pleasurable, but I learned a great amount. I served in destroyers for all the years of the war; these ships did provide young men with responsibilities very early in life. I joined the Navy with virtually no knowledge of naval matters whatsoever. It was a matter of on-the-job learning and I think that my naval experience, and having considerable responsibility—I had a full watchkeeping certificate at the age of 20—meant that I derived great benefit from my service in destroyers during the war.

I couldn't have been more fortunate in joining Shell when I came out of the Navy. It was remarkable at that time that the expansion in the oil business, perhaps particularly the marine part of the oil business, was enormous. I was very fortunate to join at a time when a lot of my seniors were approaching retirement and I found the promotion ladder suited my age very well indeed. I was there when exciting things were happening; new and bigger ships were being built all the time and it was fascinating to see what the problems were in bringing these ships into trade and dealing with all the difficulties of safety.

By far my greatest fortune was in having such a wonderful wife to share my life with. Together we have been extremely fortunate in having wonderful children. We are also fortunate in that our children have married people whom we admire very much. We take great pleasure in our extended family and we now have nine grandchildren, all of whom are adorable.

We find the part of Scotland we selected for our retirement extremely pleasant. We have made a lot of charming and delightful friends. My wife is a very keen gardener; we finished up on a north-facing rocky hillside, but she has worked very hard and has made a most attractive and beautiful garden. We are members of two golf courses, which lie within five minutes' walk of the house.

My passion, as a recreation, has been fishing. I suppose central Perthshire must be as good a place as one could find in the United

163

Kingdom, both for salmon and for trout. I start fishing my salmon right in the middle of January. On Loch Tay I have a right at the west end of the loch. I very much enjoy trolling lures around the loch in the bitter weather of January, February and March—it is quite a challenge, but it can be very beautiful. I suppose that the fishing *per se* is not very exciting: one is simply driving a boat along at about walking speed, trailing behind lures which hopefully one of the fresh run salmon will grab. The trolling of lures is not very exciting, but the scenery can be absolutely magnificent; it is wonderful to look up on a beautiful clear day to see the Bens shining white, and sometimes turning pink, in the winter sunshine. Of course, when a fish takes there is absolute pandemonium. One of the delights of fishing the Tay in the early part of the year is that the spring fish can be very large. I remember on one occasion I was out with a friend of mine in February and we hooked a 30 pound salmon. The fish was towing the boat like a tug. The weather was extremely bad; it was blowing a full gale and snowing, blizzard conditions. I was very fortunate in that my companion was a very good boatman and a very knowledgeable loch salmon fisher. He managed to keep the boat in reasonable shape while we drifted down the loch in the gale. He had a problem, because he wears glasses; his glasses were continuously covered in snow. He had great difficulty in keeping his glasses sufficiently free to see what was happening. We landed the fish a mile and a half from where it was hooked. This was nearly an hour later, by which time my arms were nearly coming out of their sockets.

Normally, I stop fishing for salmon in the loch about the middle of May and go on to trout fishing and salmon fishing in the rivers. One of the great advantages of salmon fishing in Scotland is that a number of the smaller rivers are quite delightful in terms of scenery. My wife very often joins me—she doesn't fish at all, but she enjoys the scenery and walking in the beautiful surroundings. These Highland rivers are wonderful to fish; there is no thrill like the heart stopping moment when a salmon takes your fly in a river in full spate. Then you have the dreadful problems of what to do—Should you let the fish run? Will it go downstream? If it goes downstream, you have a fair chance of losing it, because of the force of the water—unless you can run fairly fast and keep up with the fish. On the other hand, if the fish goes upstream, you have a fair chance of getting it quite easily.

One of the advantages of trout fishing over salmon fishing is that when you go fishing for salmon, you very often come back with no fish, whereas if you go trout fishing, you very seldom come back without at least one or two. In central Perthshire we are very fortunate in having some wonderful hill lochs which are very beautiful. The trout are not enormous, but they are wild brown trout, very shy and difficult to attract with a fly, but as I say, you nearly always have something, and very often have a substantial basket.

Before closing on the subject of fishing, I suppose I should mention one of my less distinguished fishing experiences. One year I kept my boat at the Kenmore end of Loch Tay, that is the east end. This is the opposite end from my fishing right and it is the end where the loch flows out and begins the River Tay. I was keeping my boat moored behind the hotel in the river, just where the river leaves the loch. It was an occasion of the French rugby international against Scotland at Murrayfield, and a bus-load of Frenchmen had come up to the village of Kenmore. I suppose there were around 60 Frenchmen; 30 of them had gone on to the golf course and the other 30 had gone onto the river. Of the 30 on the river, around 15 of them were on the hotel pool.

That particular morning, I had decided to go salmon fishing. I got my boat in the pool which is outside the hotel, at the beginning of the River Tay. I had just gone out under the bridge which takes the road over the Tay where the river meets the loch when one of my rods went with a salmon, which went roaring off down the pool. So I had a problem: I had to get the other rods in and manoeuvre the boat down the pool. I shouted out in my best French, 'J'ai un salmon', which was perfectly obvious because the fish was roaring off down the pool. The Frenchmen were kind enough to roll in the various things they were throwing into the river in the hope of attracting a fish. I got my rods in and I got the boat into the bank. One of the Frenchmen kindly took my bowline and I got out of the boat, rod in hand and went down alongside this fish, hoping to play it and land it. Unfortunately, the fish got stuck in something which was fairly deep in the water—I couldn't see what the problem was. I had completely run out of French by this time, but I asked a Frenchman to hold my rod and tried to explain by visual signs that I would have to get breast waders to go into the river and see what the trouble was and try to sort it out. My car, at this time, was over the bridge on the other side of the river, so I left the Frenchman holding the rod, got into my car and drove up to my house which is only about half a mile away. I got my breast waders, drove the car back down to the river again, got the waders on and got into the river. I could see that the line was snagged around the branch of a tree which was on the river bed. I whipped out my gaff at full extent; I was within an inch of the top of my breast waders, and I just managed to unhook the line from the branch where it was caught so that once again the salmon was swimming free. In my hurry to get ashore and get my rod to play the fish, I fell forward and filled my breast waders completely with water.

By this time, there were quite a crowd assembled on the opposite bank outside the hotel. They were shouting out that it was very early, in February, for swimming in the Tay. My breast waders were filled with extremely cold water. So, when I got onto the shore, I had to lie down on the bank and let the water flow out of my waders. I then got the rod in hand and eventually managed to land quite a large fish, but the fish was a baggot—that is, an unspawned female salmon which should not be taken; it is an unclean fish. So I tried to explain to the Frenchman, who had very kindly held my rod all this time and was very excited about what had happened, that I was going to get my pliers to unhook the fish and put it back in the water. (I use pliers, hopefully to do the minimum amount of damage to the fish.) My boat was about 20 yards further up the bank, so I went up to get my pliers when I came back, to my horror, the Frenchman had murdered the poor salmon with my gaff.

In conclusion, I hope that these ramblings will be of some interest to my family and my grandchildren, and perhaps even to one or two of my friends. As I have said many times, I believe that I have been very fortunate in having a pleasant life and good fortune.